15 Irresistible Mini-Plays For Teaching Math

BY SHERYL ANN CRAWFORD
AND NANCY I. SANDERS

SCHOLASTIC
PROFESSIONAL BOOKS

NEW YORK • TORONTO • LONDON • AUCKLAND • SYDNEY
MEXICO CITY • NEW DELHI • HONG KONG

I dedicate this book to Nancy—
my storytelling, joy-bringing, laughter-sharing,
soul-seaching, forever friend!

—S.C.

For Sherri,
who brings the gift of imagination
and the eternal sunshine of friendship into my life!
(James 1:17)

—N.S.

Cover design by Pamela Simmons
Interior design by Kathy Massaro
Cover and interior artwork by Maxie Chambliss

ISBN: 0-439-04386-7
Copyright © 1999 by Sheryl Ann Crawford and Nancy I. Sanders

Contents

☆ Introduction ☆

Imaginative play and make-believe are precious joys of childhood. These joys are often minimized, however, by the influence of television and video games. This makes it even more important to provide children with opportunities to use their imagination as they learn. Performing simple plays, whether by reading aloud or acting out a production, furnishes children with memory-building moments of creativity.

In this book, we've tried to create easy-to-read mini-plays that reinforce essential math skills, fit into your busy school day, spark the imagination, and tickle kids' funny bones. We've chosen themes that kids love, such as dinosaurs, clowns, outer space, and monsters. It is our hope that combining these well-loved themes with play-acting and hands-on math activities will appeal to children's curiosity and natural inclination to make-believe.

Children will have fun using skip counting to count chicken pox spots in "Chicken Pox Party." They'll giggle as a hungry anteater chases marching ants that have added numbers to their ranks in "Adding Ants." They'll subtract carrots with delight as forgetful rabbits dish up "Almost Carrot Stew." And along the way, you'll be able to introduce or reinforce valuable math skills that will last a lifetime.

Enjoy these plays and use them to guide children into the world of imaginative play—where mathematics comes alive!

—*Sheryl Ann Crawford and Nancy I. Sanders*

Tips for Using This Book

The 15 plays in this collection are ready to reproduce and distribute to each child in your class. You can have children read aloud the play in unison or assign parts to those children who are able to read independently. Designed for emergent readers, the plays use rhyme, repetitive language, and predictability to help children gain confidence as readers.

With younger children, you can simply read each play aloud. Some plays, such as "Adding Ants," are easy for children to memorize after hearing them several times. You might also invite those children who haven't yet mastered sufficient reading skills to act out the parts as you read the play aloud.

Following each play are suggestions for performing the play or making puppets. However, you can perform all the plays without costumes or props. Our goal is to give you options for incorporating these read-aloud plays into your classroom schedule in the manner you know works best.

Each play features one central math theme which is listed in the Contents on page 3. Use the plays to reinforce concepts you are already teaching. Activity suggestions following each play will further enhance mathematical learning while encouraging experiences such as group cooperation. The accompanying reproducibles frequently feature math manipulatives, providing young learners with hands-on experiences.

Math Standards in the Classroom

Thirteen content standards have been developed by the National Council of Teachers of Mathematics (NCTM) as the basis for teaching mathematics to children and creating a learning environment for mathematics. On the next page you will find links to the standards for each play, along with its accompanying activities. Please note that each play and its activities always represent the first four standards: Problem Solving, Communication, Reasoning, and Making Connections between mathematics and everyday life.

Connections With the NCTM Standards

	Mathematics as Problem Solving	Mathematics as Communication	Mathematics as Reasoning	Mathematical Connections	Estimation	Number Sense and Numeration	Concepts of Whole Number Operations	Whole Number Computation	Geometry and Spatial Sense	Measurement	Statistics and Probability	Fractions and Decimals	Patterns and Relationships
Five Baby Robins	✳	✳	✳	✳		✳							
Chicken Pox Party	✳	✳	✳	✳		✳		✳					✳
Clown School	✳	✳	✳	✳		✳							✳
Monster Mouth	✳	✳	✳	✳		✳		✳			✳		
Adding Ants	✳	✳	✳	✳		✳	✳	✳					
Almost Carrot Stew	✳	✳	✳	✳		✳	✳	✳					
Zooming Home	✳	✳	✳	✳						✳			
Good Morning, Dinosaurs!	✳	✳	✳	✳	✳	✳			✳	✳	✳	✳	
Jumping Contest	✳	✳	✳	✳	✳				✳	✳	✳	✳	
Little Monkey's Tick-Tock Day	✳	✳	✳	✳						✳			✳
Toy Store	✳	✳	✳	✳	✳	✳	✳	✳		✳			
Elephant Sleepover	✳	✳	✳	✳					✳			✳	✳
One Little, Two Little, Three Little Pigs	✳	✳	✳	✳				✳					✳
The Round-up	✳	✳	✳	✳				✳	✳	✳	✳		✳
Old MacDonald's Family picture	✳	✳	✳	✳							✳		✳

Five Baby Robins

(Read in unison.)

Early one morning up in a tree,
A nest of baby robins slept as quiet as can be.
Shhhh!

No baby robins chirped or peeped.
That means zero. They were all asleep.

One baby robin sat up in the nest.
He chirped out loud and woke up the rest!

Two baby robins raised their heads.
"Chirp, chirp, chirp! We want to be fed!"

Three baby robins opened wide.
"Mommy! Mommy! Feed us!" they cried.

Four baby robins began to squirm.
"It's time for breakfast! Where's our worm?"

Five baby robins cried, "Mommy's back—
with lots of worms for a tasty snack!"

One–two–three–four–five slurped and chirped.
Five baby robins ate, then burped!

"Now that you've eaten," their mommy said,
"Close your eyes and go back to bed."

Robin number five rubbed her tummy.
"Now I'm full. That sure was yummy!"

Robin number four said, "That was great!
The slimiest worm I ever ate!"

Robin number three ate too much!
"I don't think I'll be eating lunch!"

Robin number two saved a bite
to snack on later in the middle of the night.

Robin number one yawned and said,
"Mommy told us it was time for bed."

Five–four–three–two–one.
The robins are resting; their peeping is done.

No baby robins chirped or peeped.
That means zero. They were all asleep.
Shhhh!

 ☆ **The End** ☆

Five Baby Robins

Skill

Counting

Performing the Play

Use the following suggestions to perform this play with your class.

★ Have children make finger puppets and a bird-nest-bowl theater. (See instructions below.) Have children put their five finger puppets on the fingers of one hand, then slip their puppets through the bottom of the bowl so the robins are sitting in their nest. The nest can be held with the other hand. Recite the play in unison while children move the robin puppets to make them stand up or lie down.

★ Recite the play in unison, letting children perform the fingerplay motions shown on the play pages.

★ Invite a group of six children to act out the play. Let five children sit together on the floor, pretending to sleep. One by one, they wake up to eat and then go back to sleep.

Making the Puppets

Materials

★ Robin Puppet Patterns, page 11
★ crayons
★ scissors
★ tape or glue

Here's How

1 Copy and hand out the puppet patterns so that each child has one set of five puppets. Have children color the puppets and cut them out.

2 Glue or tape each puppet to fit on children's fingers.

3 Let each child make a bird-nest-bowl theater. (See next page.)

Bird-Nest-Bowl Theaters

Here's How

1 Before you distribute the bowls, cut out the bottom so that a child's hand will fit through it.

2 Give each child one bowl to decorate as a bird's nest. Have children glue 2-inch lengths of yarn and green paper leaf shapes around the top edge of the bowl. (Variation: Instead of cereal bowls, the nests can be made of brown paper lunch bags as described in Activity 1 below. The bag can be cut open to perform the play and then taped closed to complete Activity 1.

Materials

★ cardboard cereal bowl
★ brown yarn
★ green construction paper
★ scissors
★ glue

Activity 1   Build a Nest

Here's How

1 Roll down the paper bags until they're two inches high (one per child). These bags form the nests.

2 Distribute the bags to children and display the collection of nest-building supplies on a table. Invite children to come to the table and choose five objects from the collection to put in their nests.

3 Have children hold their empty nests. Ask them to count in unison up to five as they put the objects, one by one, into their nests. Then have them count in reverse order as they remove the objects from the nests.

4 After the activity, invite children to glue their objects to the nest for decoration. They can also add more leaf shapes and Plasticine eggs. By setting their finger puppets inside the nest, they have a fun centerpiece for their dinner table that encourages them to practice counting at home.

Materials

★ brown paper lunch bags
★ items that birds might put in their nests (fabric strips, pieces of yarn or string, feathers, and leaves)
★ Plasticine

Feed the Baby Birds!

Materials

* paper cups
* lightweight cardboard
* yellow, black, and brown construction paper
* pencils
* scissors
* glue

Here's How

1 Cut out several triangle patterns from lightweight cardboard, about 3 inches each. Have children use the patterns to trace and cut out two yellow paper triangles.

2 To make a beak, show them how to glue these patterns around the opening of the cup, as shown.

3 Have children each cut two circles from the black paper and glue them onto their birds to form eyes.

4 Have each child cut five 1- by 5-inch brown paper strips to represent worms. (If children are counting higher than five, they can cut out a corresponding number of worms.)

5 Ask: "How many worms did your baby bird eat?" (Encourage answers lower than the number of worms each has.) If a child answers "Four," have all children place four paper strips in the mouths of their birds (or cups), counting in unison as they do so.

6 Have children remove the worms, counting in reverse order. Repeat the question to let all children have a turn.

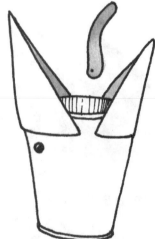

Here's More

Distribute a copy of the flip-book reproducible on page 12 to each child. Have children cut along the dotted lines and stack the pages in order from beginning to end. Staple the books together at the top. Invite children to count through the books slowly or flip through quickly to watch the baby birds wake up and go back to sleep.

Robin Puppet Patterns

Five Baby Robins

A Flip Book

Name _____

0 Zero

1 One

2 Two

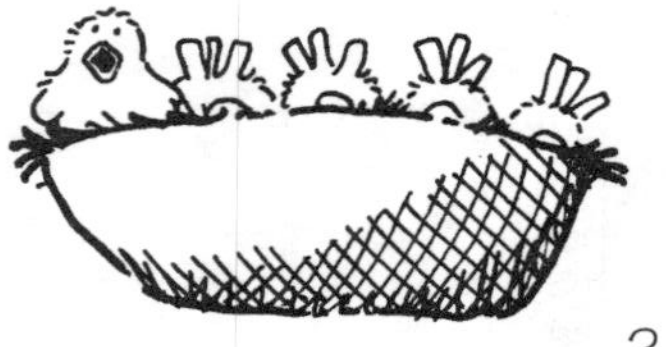

3 Three

4 Four

5 Five

1

2

3

4

5 Five

6

7

5 Five

8

4 Four

9

3 Three

10

2 Two

11

1 One

12

0 Zero

13

The End

Chicken Pox Party

Characters

Child 1, 2, 3, 4, 5, and 6
Friends

Child 1:   Since we've all got spots today,
          Let's meet at my house to play.

Child 2:   Spots on my fingers. Spots on my toes.
          I counted 10 spots on my nose.

Friends: Let's count by 2's and add those spots.
          2−4−6−8−10 red spots.
          10 red spots of chicken pox.

Child 3:   Dots on my elbows. Dots on my knees.
          Let's play dot-to-dot on me!

Child 4:   Big spots. Small spots. Pink spots. Red.
          I counted 50 on my head.

Friends: Let's count by 5's and add those spots.
5–10–15–20–25–30–35–40–45–50 spots.
50 spots of chicken pox.

Child 5: I've got spots! You've got spots.
We've got crazy polka dots!

Child 6: Itchy, itchy! Oops! Don't scratch!
Mom counted 100 on my back.

Friends: Let's count by 10's and add those spots.
10–20–30–40–50–60–70–80–90–100 spots.
100 spots of chicken pox.

All: It itches here! It itches there!
These spots are almost everywhere.
We count by 2's and 5's and 10's.
Counting spots is fun with our friends!

☆ The End ☆

Chicken Pox Party

Performing the Play

Choose six children to act out the play in front of the class. As they read their parts, encourage them to pretend to scratch and point to where they have chicken pox. The rest of the children can remain seated and read aloud the part of the "Friends."

Skill

Skip Counting

Activity 1

Crazy Dots Game

Here's How

Materials

★ chalkboard
★ chalk

1 Divide the class into four teams. Have one child from each team stand at the board and draw a crazy pattern of ten dots. Have each child label his or her own pattern of dots with skip counting by 10's from 10 to 100. There should now be four dot-to-dot patterns labeled with skip counting. These children then return to their teams.

2 Have a race in which one representative from each team steps up to the board and connects the dots in one of the patterns in proper order. (This may work best if children don't complete a pattern drawn by their own teammates.) The team that completes the pattern first scores a point.

3 This group of children stays at the board, erases the patterns, and draws a new set of ten dots. Have them label the dots with skip counting by 2's from 2 to 20.

4 Continue the game with different combinations of skip counting until every child has a turn. The team with the most points wins the game.

15

5 Challenge children to create dot-to-dot pictures using skip counting for their classmates to complete. Let children study the pictures in coloring books for ideas.

Activity 2

Skip, the Class Creature

Materials

★ Skip, the Class Creature reproducible, page 18

★ scissors

★ five sheets construction paper

★ pencils and crayons

★ four 2- by 8-inch construction paper strips

★ glue

★ craft paper

★ pushpins

★ stapler or clear tape

Here's How

1 Give each child a copy of the reproducible page. Children can work in groups: One group will make hair for Skip; another group will make Skip's eyes; and a third will make shoes for Skip to wear.

2 Assign five children to be in the group that makes Skip's hair. Each child cuts out a hair pattern from a sheet of constuction paper, so that there will be five groups of ten strands of hair. The strips can be rolled around a pencil or accordion-folded, as the child prefers.

3 Assign four children to be in the group that makes Skip's shoes. Each child makes one set of five shoes for Skip so that there are four groups of five shoes each. Glue one 2- by 8-inch strip of construction paper to each group of shoes to represent Skip's legs.

4 The rest of the children make 25 pairs of eyes for Skip. Have them color in black dots for the center of each eye. Some children might make two pairs of eyes.

5 Cut a large shape from butcher paper as shown in the illustration. It should measure at least 3 feet wide by 2 feet high. Hang this shape on the bulletin board.

6 Help children staple the hair, eyes, and shoes on Skip, as shown. When children return to their seats, have them count Skip's hair by skip counting by 10's. Then have them count his eyes by skip counting by 2's and, finally, his shoes by 5's.

Skip, the Class Creature

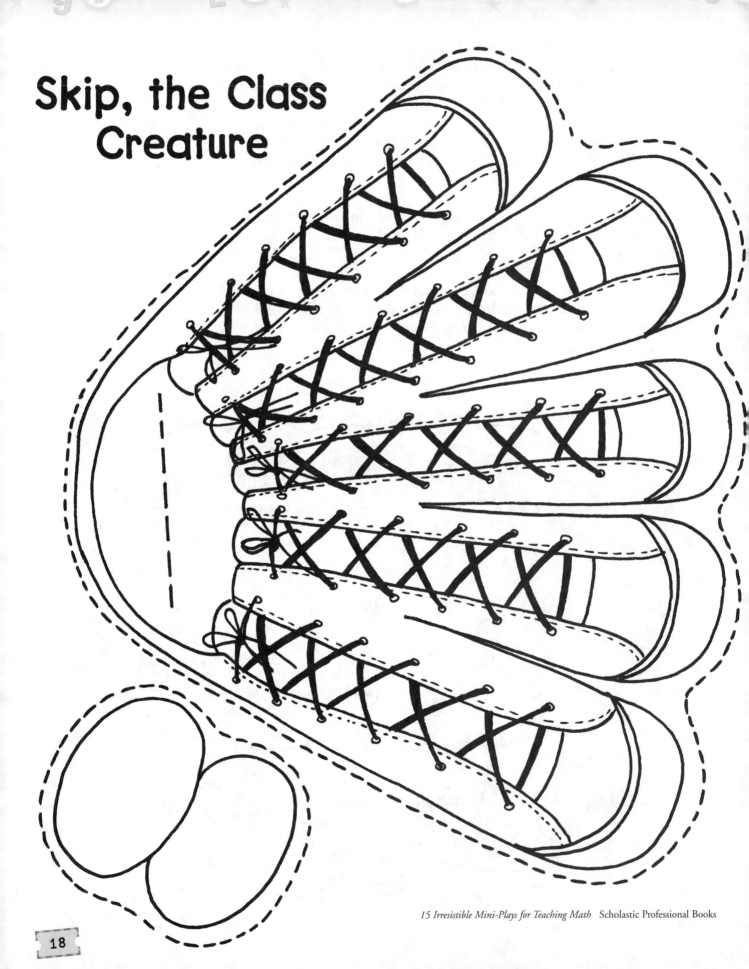

Clown School

Characters

Mr. Clown
Mrs. Clown
Clown Child 1
Clown Child 2
Clown Child 3

Mr. and Mrs. Clown: It's time to get ready for Clown School!

Clown Child 1: First, we'll eat breakfast.

Clown Child 2: Second, we'll put on our clown clothes.

Clown Child 3: Third, we'll leave for Clown School.

Mr. and Mrs. Clown: Last, you'll come home again!

Clown Child 1: First, we'll eat our oatmeal.

All Clown Children: We're clowns. Let's juggle our breakfast dishes!

⟶

Clown Child 2:   Second, we'll put on our clown clothes.

All Clown Children: We're clowns. We like to dress silly!

Clown Child 3:   Third, we'll leave for Clown School.

All Clown Children: We're clowns.
We learn to be funny at Clown School!

Mr. and Mrs. Clown: Last, it will be time to come home again!

All Clown Children: We're home!

Mr. and Mrs. Clown: It's time to do your homework!

Clown Child 1:   First, we'll blow up BIG balloons.

Clown Child 2:   Second, we'll honk our funny horns.

Clown Child 3:   Third, we'll make silly faces! ⟶

Mr. and Mrs. Clown: Last, it will be time to eat dinner
and then go to bed.

Clown Child 1: First, we'll eat our dinner.

All Clown Children: We're clowns.
Let's spin our dinner dishes!

Clown Child 2: Second, we'll put on our funny pajamas.

All Clown Children: We're clowns.
We dress silly even when we go to bed!

Clown Child 3: Third, we'll turn out the light.

All Clown Children: We're clowns.
We get our rest to do our best
in Clown School!

Mr. and Mrs. Clown: Last of all, we'll say good night.

All: May we honk our horns in bed?

Mr. and Mrs. Clown: Of course! You're clowns. Good night!

☆ **The End** ☆

Clown School

Skill

Order of Events

Performing the Play

Use the following suggestions to perform this play with your class.

★ To act out this play, first enlarge and photocopy the bow tie and nose patterns on page 23. The tie and nose can be taped on after they are colored and cut out. You can perform the part of the clown parents or let children volunteer. Have three children dress in costume and stand in front of the class to read their dialogue. For added fun, use props, such as bike horns, balloons, paper bowls, and paper plates!

★ Have children sit at their seats and read the play aloud. You may read the parts of Mr. and Mrs. Clown or assign a pair of children to read their lines. From their seats, children can go through the motions of waking up, putting on clown outfits, and eating breakfast. They can pretend to walk to Clown School and home again by stomping their feet in place. At the end of the play, children all pretend to honk silly bicycles horns.

Activity 1

In What Order Did It Happen?

Materials

★ In What Order Did It Happen? reproducible, page 24

★ crayons

★ scissors

★ stapler

Here's How

1 Give each child a copy of the reproducible. Have children cut apart the three pictures for the story "The Circus." Give them time to determine the order of events. Then ask them to write 1, 2, or 3 in each circle and color the pictures.

2 Ask volunteers to explain their reasoning in determining the order of the pictures. Have children check each other, then staple the three-page story together to make a mini-book.

3 Repeat the activity with the story "Clowns." As a variation, review the ordinal numbers used in the play and have children write *first*, *second*, or *third* in the circle on each page.

Activity 2

What Happens Next?

Here's How

1 Divide the class into four groups. Have one group draw trees with only blossoms. Have the second group draw trees with green leaves. Have the third group draw trees with brown or yellow leaves falling to the ground. Have the fourth group draw trees with bare branches.

2 Talk with children about the seasons in a forest. Have the first group stand up and display their pictures of trees with blossoms. Explain that in the spring, first the trees grow blossoms. Ask children to suggest other things that happen first during the spring. Children might suggest that baby animals are born or that flowers start to grow. Then have that group sit down.

3 Have each consecutive group stand up and display their pictures, showing what happens next to trees in the forest. Encourage children to continue the discussion about other things that happen next in the forest.

4 After every group has shared its pictures, ask children to list what happened first, second, third, and last in the forest.

Here's More

Encourage children to tell stories about the order of events. Give them story prompts, such as "The farmer planted seeds," "The children bought tickets to see the circus," "Grandpa decided to bake cookies," or "The bear woke up from hibernating all winter." Let different children each add a single event to the story. As children tell the story, encourage them to say "first," second," "third," and "last."

Materials

★ drawing paper
★ crayons

Bow-tie Pattern

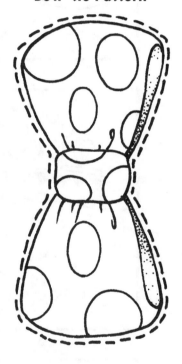

Nose Pattern

In What Order Did It Happen?

☆ The Circus ☆

☆ Clowns ☆

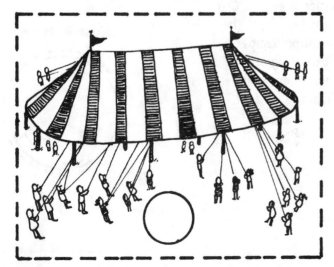

15 Irresistible Mini-Plays for Teaching Math   Scholastic Professional Books

Monster Mouth

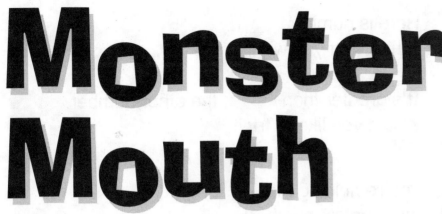

Characters

Monster Mouth   Child 2
Child 1   Class

Monster Mouth: My name is Monster Mouth.
I have an empty tummy.
I've heard this class has lots of numbers,
Numbers that are yummy!

Child 1:
(holding smaller
number)
My number is ☐, Monster Mouth.
Will it fit into your tummy?
I know that it's less than the number ☐,
But won't it taste just as yummy?

Monster Mouth: Your number is a nice one,
But I'd rather eat another.
I only eat the greatest number,
Not one that is less than the other. ⟶

25

Child 2:
(holding larger
number)

Here is number ☐.
I think that you will like it.

It's greater than ☐, the other number.
Would you like to try it?

Monster Mouth:

You're holding the ☐,
the greatest number!
It's greater than the other.
I can't wait another minute.
It's making my monster mouth water!

Class:

His name is Monster Mouth.
Our numbers are good to eat.
He gobbles the greatest numbers.
The bigger, the better,
is his kind of treat!

☆ **The End** ☆

Monster Mouth

Performing the Play

Write a selection of numbers on large index cards, one number per card. Use a black marker to make them large and easy to see. Choose three students to perform the play. Have one child wear the Monster Mouth puppet. (You can make one puppet for children to take turns using, or children can use puppets they've made.) Let the other two children each pick an index card with a number on it.

The performers come to the front of the room. Give them time to determine which student is holding the greatest number and which is holding the least. They will then read the part that corresponds to the relationship between the numbers they are holding. Students will say the name of their number instead of the blank box in the text of the play. At the end of the play, Monster Mouth pretends to eat the greater number. This play can be performed over and over again until every child gets a turn to perform.

Making the Puppet

Here's How

1 Cut one paper plate in half. Staple the two halves to the second plate as shown so that the bottoms of the plates face out. Put tape over the staples to cover sharp edges. (Optional: Paint the puppet.)

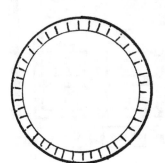 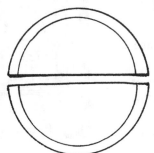 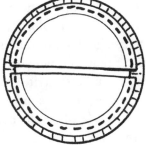

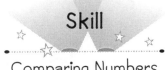

Skill

Comparing Numbers

Materials

★ 2 dinner-sized paper plates
★ jumbo cotton balls
★ black construction paper
★ scissors
★ stapler
★ tape
★ paint and paintbrushes (optional)

2 Using the illustrations as a guide, glue two cotton balls to the puppet for eyes. Glue two black construction paper circles to the front of the cotton ball eyes.

3 Have children wear the puppet on one hand and use their fingers to open and close its mouth.

Favorite Foods Graph

Materials

★ construction paper
★ crayons or markers

Here's How

1 Discuss with children the kind of food they most like to gobble up. Then ask everyone to draw a picture of a favorite food.

2 Create a large graph on a bulletin board. Make at least three columns, as shown. Mount each child's picture on the bulletin board in the appropriate column.

3 Let children study the graph. Then discuss which column has the greatest number of items. Compare the number of items in each column, discussing which numbers are greater than and which are less than the others. Invite children to write expressions of inequality (< >) on the board corresponding to the relationship of the number of items displayed in each column. Ask which numbers Monster Mouth would like to eat.

Let's Feed Monster Mouth!

Here's How

1 Give each child an assortment of counters and a copy of the reproducible.

2 Ask two volunteers to each name a number. (Make sure the numbers add up to less than the number of counters each child has.)

3 Have children count out two piles of counters representing the two numbers. Tell them to place the counters for the larger number on the plate facing Monster Mouth. Place the counters for the smaller number on the other plate.

4 Repeat the activity as often as you like.

Materials

★ Let's Feed Monster Mouth reproducible, page 30
★ math counters

Here's More

1 Give children time to walk around the classroom, collecting an assortment of small objects. Tell them that they may collect only as many objects as they can carry at once, but they may collect as few as they want. After children return to their seats with their collection, have them count the number of objects they collected.

2 Choose two volunteers to count their objects for the class. Ask them to determine who has the greatest number and who has the least number of objects. Write the inequality expression on the chalkboard. Continue asking pairs of children about the number of objects in their collection until every child has had a turn. Give children time to return their objects to where they belong.

Let's Feed Monster Mouth

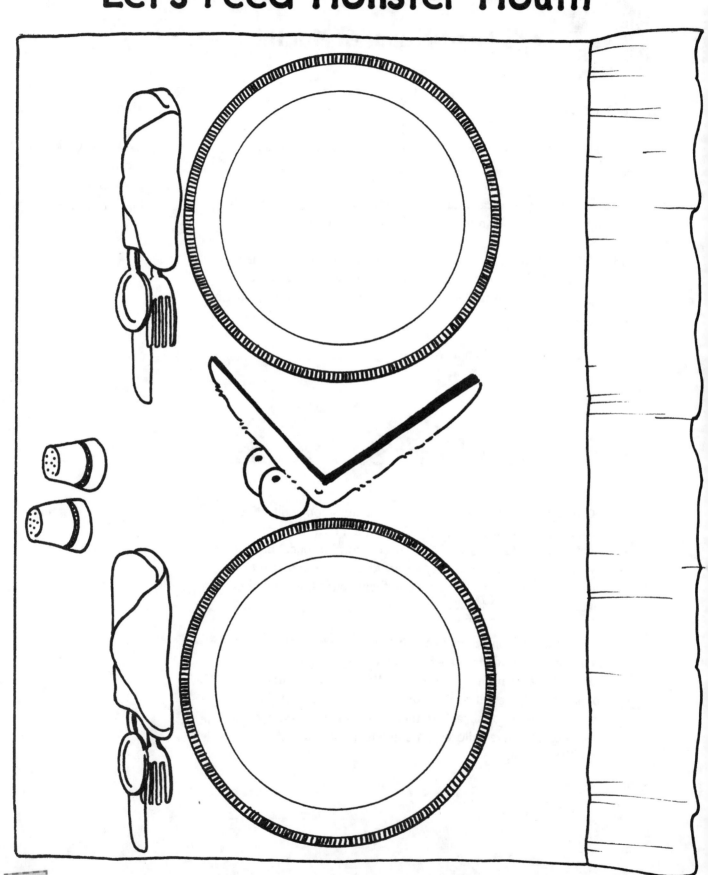

Adding Ants

Characters

Ants 1 to 10
Anteater
Chorus

Ants 1 to 3:   One little, two little, three little ants
went marching in the morning.

Ants 4 to 5:   Two ants sitting on a rock said,
"We're coming too!"

Chorus: Three ants plus two ants
equal five ants marching in the morning.
One little, two little, three little,
four little, five little ants
went marching in the morning.

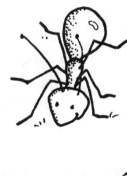

Ants 6 to 10:   Five ants peeked out from an anthill.
"We're coming too!" they said.
Five ants plus five more ants
equal ten ants marching in the morning.

Chorus: One little, two little, three little,
four little, five little, six little,
seven little, eight little, nine little,
ten little ants marching in the morning.

Anteater: Out from behind a tree popped an anteater!
"I'm coming too!"
Ten little ants plus one anteater
equal ten little ants running everywhere!

Chorus: Plus one hungry anteater!

☆ **The End** ☆

Adding Ants

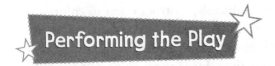

Performing the Play

Use the following suggestions to perform this play with your class.

★ Read the play aloud with your class while they sit at their desks. Children may stomp their feet in place to sound like marching ants. When the 10 ants run, tell them to stomp their feet very quickly.

★ Ask 11 volunteers to act out the play. The first three ants march around the room. The next set of ants sit on a brown sheet of craft paper representing a log. The next set hide behind a chair covered with a sheet or brown paper to represent the anthill. At the end of the play, the 10 children can all run back to their seats when they see the hungry anteater.

Thumbprint Ant Addition

Here's How

1 Give each child a sheet of paper. Use smaller pieces of paper or an index card with young children.

2 Let children make as many thumbprints on their papers as they want, using the stamp pad or paint. Older children can make a larger number of ants. When the ink or paint has dried, encourage children to draw legs and silly faces on their thumbprints so they resemble ants.

3 Have children join up with a partner and add together the ants in their pictures. Ask children to write their addition equations on the back of their pictures.

4 Switch partners and repeat the addition activity as often as you want.

Skill

Addition

Materials

★ index cards or white paper
★ black stamp pads or black paint
★ fine-tipped markers or pens

Adding More Ants

Here's How

1 Give children each a copy of the reproducible. Instruct them to color five ants red and five black and then cut out all 10 ants. (If you want children to practice adding numbers higher than 10, reproduce as many ants as you'd like for them to use as manipulatives. Have them color half the ants red and half black.)

2 Give children different word problems, such as "Three red ants and four black ants went marching down the road." Tell children to place the appropriate number of ants in each square. Encourage them to count each group of ants.

3 Have each child tape together the two halves of a sheet of of black construction paper, end to end, to create a "road." After everyone has the correct number of ants in each square, instruct children to place both groups on the black paper road in one long line, end to end. Then count the line of ants aloud in unison. (If children are counting numbers higher than 10, they can make longer roads by taping together narrow strips of black paper end to end.)

4 Repeat the addition activity, asking children to suggest different numbers of red and black ants that marched down the road.

Here's More

Have children play an addition game. Supply a group of two to four children with a pair of number cubes and math counters or duplicated ants from the Adding More Ants reproducible on page 35. (Have younger children use only one number cube.) To play the game, put all the counters or ants in the center of the group. The first player rolls the number cube and takes that number of counters or ants. The next player takes a turn and collects the number of manipulatives shown on the cube. The players continue in turn, rolling the cube and taking the corresponding number of counters or ants. The winner is the first player who collects 10, 25, 50, 100, or any other number of ants you have determined beforehand.

Materials

★ Adding More Ants reproducible, page 35

★ red and black crayons

★ scissors

★ black construction paper, cut in half lengthwise

Adding More Ants

Red Ants	Black Ants

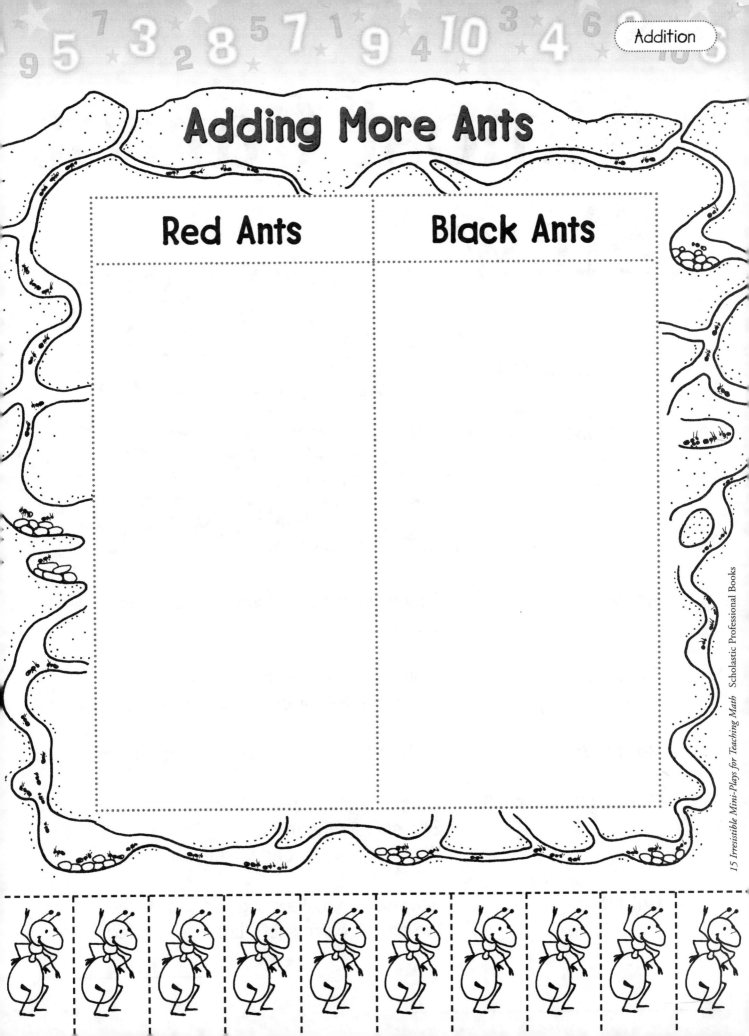

Almost Carrot Stew

Characters

Rabbit 1   Rabbit 3
Rabbit 2

Rabbit 1:   Today we make our great carrot stew!
                           We have 10 carrots. Let's get started.

Rabbit 2:   Wait. First we must bake a cake.
                           A carrot cake for our cousin's birthday.

Rabbit 3:   Right! We'll need 5 carrots for carrot cake.

Rabbits 1, 2, and 3:   Chop, chop, chop the 5 carrots.
                           Stir, stir, stir the mix.
                           Pour it in the pan and bake!

Rabbit 1:   Now we can make our great carrot stew!
                           We have 5 carrots left. Let's get started.

Rabbit 2: Wait. First we must peel carrot sticks.
Our other cousin needs them for her lunch.

Rabbit 3: Right! We'll need 2 carrots.

Rabbits 1, 2, and 3: Peel, peel, peel the 2 carrots.
Chop, chop, chop them into carrot sticks.

Rabbit 1: Now we can make our great carrot stew!
We have 3 carrots left. Let's get started.

Rabbit 2: Wait. First we must make boiled carrots.
Grandma Rabbit eats them for her lunch.

Rabbit 3: Right! We'll need 3 carrots for that.

Rabbits 1, 2, and 3: Chop, chop, chop the 3 carrots.
Boil, boil, boil them in the water.

Rabbit 1: Now we can make our great carrot stew!
Wait! We have no carrots left!

Rabbit 2:

We had 10 carrots. Now we have zero!
How will we make our carrot stew?

Rabbit 3:

I just thought of a new recipe!
Boil, boil, boil the water in the pot.
Shake, shake, shake in the salt and pepper.
Stir, stir, stir in the potatoes and cabbage.

Rabbits 1 and 2:

What is it? It smells great!

Rabbit 3:

We almost had 10 carrots for our stew,
so I call it Almost Carrot Stew!

Rabbits 1, 2, and 3:

Yum. Yum. Yum.
We can almost taste the carrots.

☆ **The End** ☆

Almost Carrot Stew

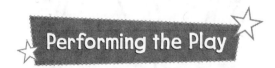

Performing the Play

Use the following suggestions to perform this play with your class.

★ Have three children read aloud the play as they hold their rabbit puppets. (See instructions below.)

★ Divide the class into three groups. One group reads the part of each rabbit.

★ Perform the play with three children acting as the rabbits. Props for this play include carrots, cooking utensils, and pans. Costumes may include simple paper bunny-ear headbands for each rabbit. As children perform the play, they can pretend to cook each dish and put the correct number of carrots in each pan.

Making the Puppets

Here's How

1 Use the Rabbit Ear Patterns on page 40 to make several cardboard templates for children to trace and cut out from white paper.

2 Glue the two white pompoms as cheeks and the pink pompom as a nose onto the back bowl of the spoon, as shown. Glue on the two plastic eyes. (Optional: You may substitute paper eyes, cheeks, and nose.)

3 Glue the ears to the end of the spoon, as shown.

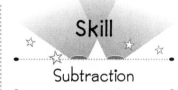
Skill

Subtraction

Materials

★ cardboard
★ white plastic spoon
★ Rabbit Ear Patterns, page 40
★ white construction paper
★ scissors
★ two 1/2-inch white pompoms
★ one 1/4-inch pink pompom
★ two 1/2-inch plastic moveable eyes (available at craft stores)
★ glue

Rabbit Ear Patterns

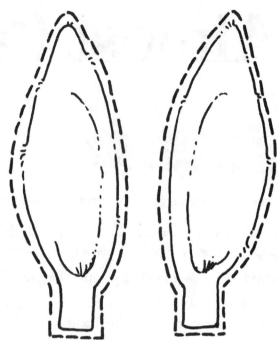

Cooking With Carrots

Materials

★ Cooking With Carrots reproducible, page 42

★ crayons

★ scissors

Here's How

1 Give each child a copy of the reproducible to color. Have children cut out the carrots to use as manipulatives. (If you are subtracting from numbers higher than 10, make additional copies of the carrots for each child to cut out.)

2 As you read the play aloud, ask children to place the correct number of carrots on each picture at corresponding points in the play.

3 Afterward, ask children questions such as, "If the rabbits used eight carrots in the cake, how many carrots would be left to use in the stew?"

4 Instruct children to place eight carrots on the picture of the cake and the remainder on the picture of the pot. Ask, "How many carrots are left?"

5 Continue asking different questions, using a different number of carrots for each dish. Always ask how many carrots would be left to use in the stew. Have children place the carrots on the reproducible as you pose the questions.

How Many Carrots?

Here's How

1 Divide the class into groups. Give each child one sheet of orange construction paper. Have children cut the paper in half lengthwise and then cut each piece into strips. Size isn't important. Have children pile all the strips of paper in the center of each group. Each strip represents one carrot.

2 Present subtraction problems to children and have each group use the paper strips as manipulatives to solve the problem. For example, say, "We have 28 carrots." Have each group count out 28 strips of paper. Then say, "If we subtract 12 carrots, how many carrots will your group have left over to put in the stew?"

3 Allow time for the groups to count out the paper strips. Choose a representative from one of the groups to put the correct number of carrots in the cooking pot.

4 Repeat the activity as often as you like. Each subtraction problem may also be written on the board as it is completed correctly.

Materials

★ large cooking pot
★ orange construction paper
★ scissors

Here's More

Have a small feast in class. Ask each child to bring in a recipe made from carrots, such as carrot muffins, carrot salad, carrot sticks with vegetable dip, and "ants on a log" (carrot sticks spread with peanut butter). Tell children to be prepared to share the number of carrots it took to make their recipes. Provide a stew or vegetable soup as the main course—but don't put any carrots in the stew.

Before you eat, ask children to share the number of carrots their recipes used. Write the total number on the board. One by one, subtract the number of carrots used for each dish. You should end up with zero. Explain that since there are no more carrots left, the class will also be eating Almost Carrot Stew—stew with no carrots in it!

Safety Note Before doing this activity, check with parents about any possible food allergies your students might have.

Cooking With Carrots

15 Irresistible Mini-Plays for Teaching Math   Scholastic Professional Books

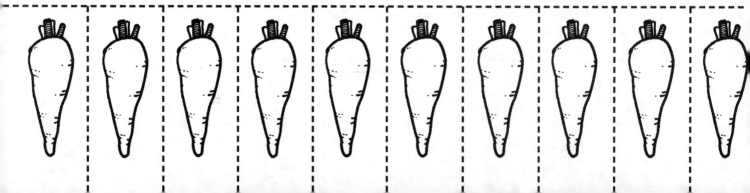

Zooming Home

Characters

Narrator	Trina Triangle
Sarah Circle	Tony Triangle
Steven Square	Ryan Rectangle
Sonia Square	Rosa Rectangle

Narrator: Zoom! Zoom! Zoom!
Sarah Circle's spaceship blasted through outer space.

Sarah Circle: Boo-hoo! I'm lost. Where's my planet?

Narrator: Sarah Circle saw a planet shaped like a square.
She blasted down for a landing.

Sarah Circle: Is this my home?

Steven Square: Welcome to Planet Square.
All our trees are square.

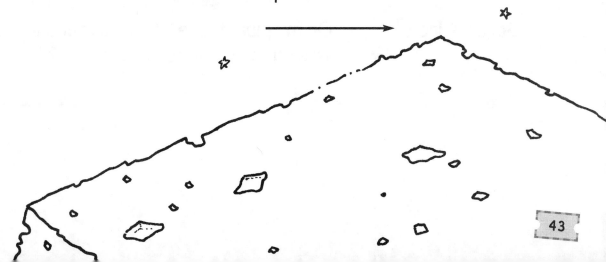

Sonia Square: All our houses are square.
All our people are square.
Even our pets are square.

**Steven and
Sonia Square:**   We love squares!

Sarah Circle: Everything here has four sides
that are all the same length.

Steven Square: Everything here has four corners.

Sarah Circle: On my planet, everything is round like a ball.
This can't be my home. Good-bye!

→

Narrator: Zoom! Zoom! Zoom!
Sarah Circle's spaceship blasted through
outer space.

Sarah Circle: Boo-hoo! I'm lost. Where's my planet?

Narrator: Sarah Circle saw a planet shaped like a triangle.
She blasted down for a landing.

Sarah Circle: Is this my home?

Trina Triangle: Welcome to Planet Triangle.
All our trees are triangles.

Tony Triangle: All our houses are triangles.
All our people are triangles.
Even our pets are triangles.

**Trina and Tony
Triangle:** We love triangles!

Sarah Circle: Everything here has three straight sides.

Trina Triangle: Everything here has three corners.

Sarah Circle: On my planet, everything is round like a ball.
This can't be my home. Good-bye!

Narrator:	Zoom! Zoom! Zoom! Sarah Circle's spaceship blasted through outer space.
Sarah Circle:	Boo-hoo! I'm lost. Where's my planet?
Narrator:	Sarah Circle saw a planet shaped like a rectangle. She blasted down for a landing.
Sarah Circle:	Is this my home?
Ryan Rectangle:	Welcome to Planet Rectangle. All our trees are rectangles.
Rosa Rectangle:	All our houses are rectangles. All our people are rectangles. Even our pets are rectangles.
Ryan and Rosa Rectangle:	We love rectangles!
Sarah Circle:	Everything here has four straight sides, and two of the sides are longer than the others.
Ryan Rectangle:	Everything here has four corners.
Sarah Circle:	On my planet, everything is round like a ball. This can't be my home. Good-bye!

Narrator:	Zoom! Zoom! Zoom! Sarah Circle's spaceship blasted through outer space.
Sarah Circle:	Boo-hoo! I'm lost. Where's my planet?
Narrator:	Sarah Circle saw a planet shaped like a circle! She blasted down for a landing.
Sarah Circle:	Wow! All the trees are round! All the houses are round! All the people are round! Even the pets are round! Everything here is round like a ball—just like me! Look! Here's my round dog, Dot! Now I know I'm home! No more zooming around! I'm back on Planet Circle!

☆ The End ☆

Zooming Home

Shapes

Skill

Shapes

Materials

★ construction paper in different colors

★ scissors

★ crayons

★ craft sticks

★ glue or tape

Performing the Play

Use the following suggestions to perform this play with your class.

★ Choose four volunteers to stand at the side of the bulletin board.

★ Divide the rest of the class into pairs or groups of three (depending on your class size). Assign each pair or group a different character's part to recite in unison as the volunteers move the puppets accordingly in front of the bulletin board. (See instructions below.)

★ Perform the play as a group with children seated at their desks. Distribute a copy of the Zooming Home reproducible on page 51 to each child. Children will use them as story mats. As you read the play aloud, children pick up the appropriate puppets and move them around on the corresponding shapes on their story mats.

Making the Puppets

Here's How

1 Cut out construction paper squares, triangles, rectangles, and circles. Make enough so that each child has one of each shape.

2 Invite children to draw features on their shapes, then glue or tape each to a craft stick to form a stick puppet.

Building the Bulletin Board Theater

Here's How

Materials

★ craft paper (dark blue and other colors)

★ scissors

★ stapler

★ star stickers

1 Cover the bulletin board with dark blue craft paper to represent outer space. Cut out a large circle, square, triangle, and rectangle in contrasting colors. Mount these shapes on the board, as shown on the next page. Label each planet accordingly. Write "Zooming Home" in large letters on a piece of construction paper or use ready-made cut-out letters.

2 Cut out a variety of small (about 2 inches) and large (about 4 inches) shapes, representing all four shapes in both sizes. Distribute these randomly to children. On these shapes, the children may draw houses, birds, cars, and so on. Mount the shapes on their matching planets.

3 Decorate the board with star stickers. Invite children to create spaceships by combining different shapes, then mount these on the board as well.

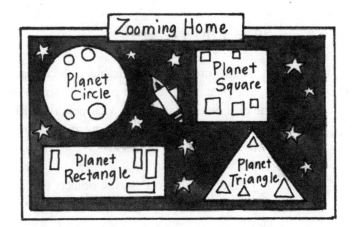

Zooming Home

Planet Circle

Planet Square

Planet Rectangle

Planet Triangle

Activity 1

Four Shapes Game

Here's How

1 Use craft paper to make a large circle, triangle, square, and rectangle. Hang each of the shapes on a wall in your classroom. Write the name of each shape on an index card and put these four cards into a paper bag.

2 To play the game, have children stand near the shape of their choice. Pull out one index card from the bag and read it aloud. Children standing next to that shape are now out of the game and sit down. Put the card back into the bag and have the remaining children move or stay near the shape of their choice. When only two players remain, each child must choose a different shape to stand next to. Repeat this activity until there is only one child left. The winner becomes the next person to pick the cards out of the bag. (Note: Toward the end of the game, you may remove two of the cards from the bag and only work with two shapes.)

3 Make the game more challenging by adding other shapes, for example, different kinds of triangles (equilateral, isosceles, and so on), hexagons, and ovals.

Materials

★ craft paper
★ scissors
★ stapler or tape
★ index cards
★ small paper bag
★ marker

Activity 2

Planet Shapes

Materials

★ Zooming Home story mat, page 51
★ pencils
★ scissors
★ glue

Here's How

1 Distribute the reproducible. Ask children to describe the shape of one of the planets. After that planet has been described, have children trace over the outline of that planet with pencils. After you discuss each of the shapes, have children cut out the items at the bottom of the page and glue them onto the matching planet.

2 Ask children to describe objects they see in the classroom that have a distinct shape. Let them determine which planets these objects should go on.

Here's More

You can make centers in the classroom that represent the shapes of the four different planets in the play. On pieces of construction paper, draw a circle, square, triangle, and rectangle. Place one sign in each center. Invite children to find items in the room or bring several items from home that have any of these shapes. Have them bring the items to the centers and display them on the matching "planets."

Zooming Home

Planet Circle

Planet Rectangle

Planet Square

Planet Triangle

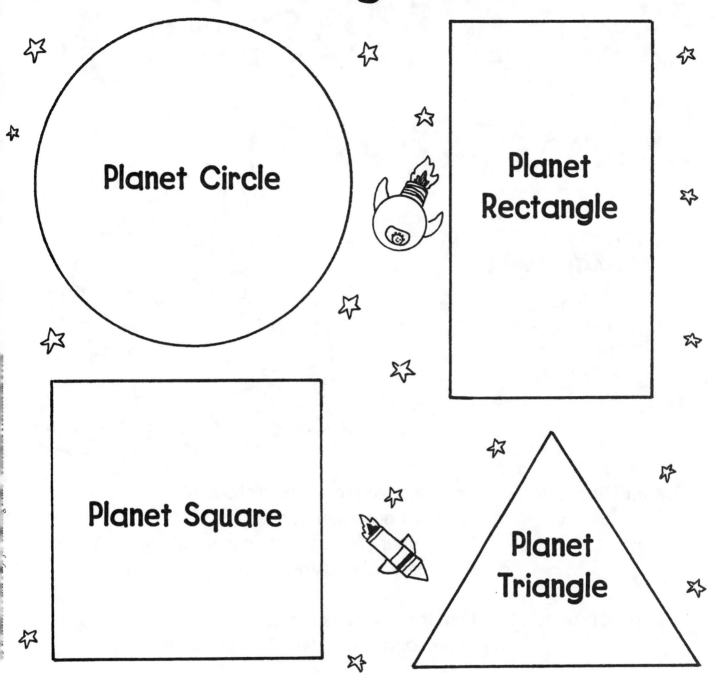

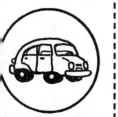

Good Morning, Dinosaurs!

Characters

Mom Dinosaur
Small Dinosaur
Medium Dinosaur
Big Dinosaur

Mom Dinosaur:
Good morning my three dinosaurs!
You must not sleep till noon.
Put on your slippers, put on your robes,
And come to breakfast soon.

Small Dinosaur:
I am the smallest dinosaur.
I yawn and stretch with a small-sounding roar.
Roar!

Medium Dinosaur:
I am the medium-sized dinosaur.
I yawn and stretch with a medium-sized roar.
R-O-A-R!

Big Dinosaur:
I am the biggest dinosaur.
I yawn and stretch with the biggest roar.
R - O - A - R!

Small Dinosaur: These are my slippers.
The size is just right,
Not too big and not too tight.
This is my robe. I know it is mine.
It's small like me. It fits me just fine!

Medium Dinosaur: These are my slippers.
Everyone knows that medium-sized slippers
Don't pinch my toes.
This is my robe, the medium-sized one.
I slip in my arms, tie the belt, and I'm done!

Big Dinosaur: These are my slippers, the biggest size,
With room to wiggle my toes inside.
Here is my robe. I don't have to hunt.
It covers me up from my back to my front!

Small Dinosaur: I have an idea! Let's trade slippers and robes.
It might be fun! Let's see how it goes.

Medium Dinosaur: The biggest slippers fall off my feet!
The robe hangs down like a great big sheet!

Big Dinosaur: These small slippers are much too snug!
The robe will tear if I pull or tug!

Small Dinosaur: These medium-sized slippers slide and slip.
The robe hits the floor. One step, it could rip!

Medium Dinosaur: That idea was not good.
Let's wear the right sizes.
When Mom sees us at breakfast,
There will be no surprises!

Mom Dinosaur: Here you are, my dinosaurs,
Your eggs and toast are done.

Small Dinosaur: What do you think about trading food?
Who knows—it might be fun!

Medium and Big Dinosaurs: No way! R-O-A-R!

☆ **The End** ☆

54

Good Morning, Dinosaurs!

Performing the Play

Use the following suggestions to perform this play with your class.

★ Perform the play as a class. Have children recite the dialogue in unison and hold up the appropriate puppet for each character. (There is no puppet for the mother dinosaur.)

★ Choose four children to perform the play for the class. Try to pick three children of noticeably different sizes for the dinosaur children. For added fun, use bathrobes and slippers of different sizes as props!

Making the Puppets

Here's How

Distribute a puppet pattern page to each child. Have children color the puppets, cut them out, and glue each puppet to a craft stick.

Activity 1

What Size Breakfast?

Here's How

1 Ask children to describe the size of breakfast and the kind of food they imagine each dinosaur would eat. Then give each child a copy of the Dinosaur Puppet Pattern page. Have children color the dinosaurs and cut them out.

2 Distribute a copy of the What Size Breakfast? reproducible to each child. Have children trace each dinosaur onto the page, covering as many breakfasts as possible with each. (The dinosaurs might overlap.)

Skill

ComparingSizes

Materials

★ Dinosaur Puppet Patterns, page 57
★ craft sticks
★ crayons
★ scissors
★ glue

Materials

★ What Size Breakfast? reproducible, page 58
★ Dinosaur Puppet Patterns, page 57
★ crayons
★ scissors
★ pencils

3 Ask children to count the breakfasts that fit inside each dinosaur. As a
class, determine the number that best fit in the smallest dinosaur, the
medium-sized dinosaur, and the biggest dinosaur. Compare the numbers
and discuss the relationship between their sizes.

Activity 2 — Wearing the Best Sizes

Materials

★ craft paper for bulletin board

★ Dinosaur Puppet Patterns, page 57

★ Robe and Slippers Patterns, page 59

★ scissors

★ crayons

★ stapler

Here's How

1 Give each child a copy of the Robe
and Slippers Pattern page. Ask children
to choose one pair of slippers and a robe
to color and cut out.

2 Make a chart on the bulletin board,
as shown. Enlarge the puppet
reproducible to add dinosaur pictures at
the top of the graph.

3 Let children take turns bringing their paper robes and slippers up to the
graph and determining where they should be placed. Staple them to the
board.

4 Discuss the various sizes children chose. Count and compare the number
of robes and slippers of each size that are displayed on the board.

Here's More

Create a center for classifying sizes. On a table, gather an
assortment of objects in three different sizes, such as three
blocks, three leaves, and three toy cars. Tape three signs on the
table: Small, Medium, and Big. Give children time to visit the
center and explore the sizes of the objects. Encourage them to
classify matching objects according to size by placing them on
the appropriate signs. Children can also classify unrelated
objects according to size.

Dinosaur Puppet Patterns

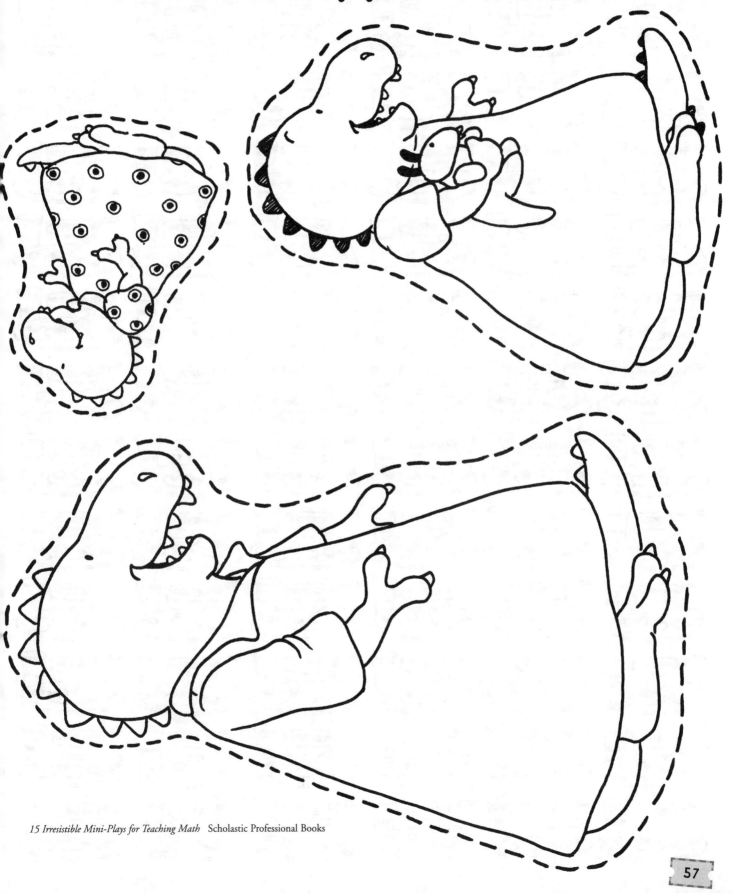

What Size Breakfast?

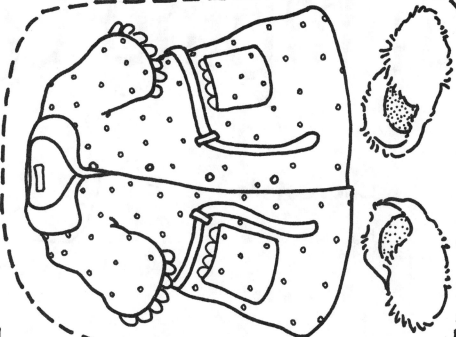

Robe and Slippers Patterns

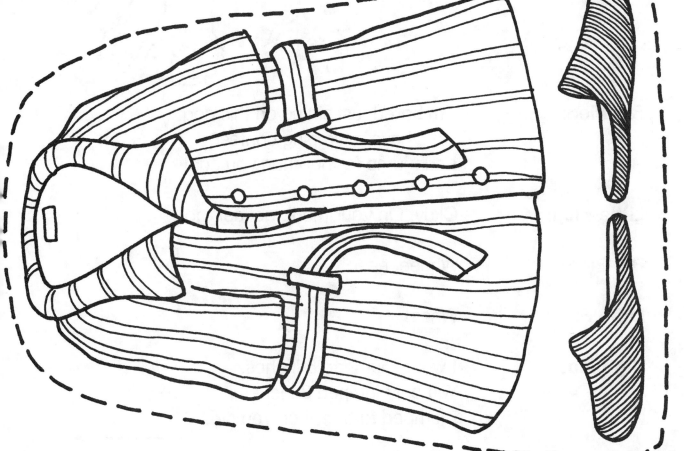

Jumping Contest

Characters

Big Flea
Little Flea

Big Flea: I'm bored just sitting on this dog.
Let's have a jumping contest.
I can jump farther than you can!

Little Flea: Okay. On your mark, get set, go!

Big Flea: Wheeeeeeee!

Little Flea: Whee!

Big Flea: I won! I jumped 5 inches.
You only jumped 3 inches.
I jumped farther than you did.

Little Flea: Let's try again.

Big Flea: Okay. But I'll win.

Little Flea: On your mark, get set, go!

Big Flea: Wheeeeeeee!

Little Flea: Whee!

Big Flea: I won again! I jumped 6 inches.
You only jumped 2 inches.

Little Flea: Let's try one more time.

Big Flea: Okay. But I'll win again.
My legs are longer, and I can jump farther.
On your mark, get set, go!

Big Flea: Wheeeeeeee!

Little Flea: Look out! Here comes the dog's paw!
It's going to scratch right on top of me!
Jump for your life!
Wheeeeeeeeeeeeeeeeeeeeeeeee!

Big Flea: Wow! Look how far you jumped!
You jumped 12 inches! I only jumped 5 inches.

Little Flea: I won! Now I'm ready for the Flea Olympics!

☆ **The End** ☆

Jumping Contest

Skill

Measuring Distance

Performing the Play

This play can be read aloud by children at their seats, or two children can perform the parts of the fleas, jumping as indicated. Children may jump different distances than those specified in the text, but Big Flea should jump farther the first two times. Little Flea should jump farthest at the end of the play. (Optional: Use correction fluid to mask the measurements given in the play. Write in the numbers you want to use and then photocopy the revised reproducibles.)

Activity 1

The Jumping Flea

Materials

★ The Jumping Flea reproducible, page 64

★ 12-inch rulers

★ pencils

Here's How

1 Give each child a copy of the reproducible and a ruler.

2 Have children measure from the dog to the mouse and record the distance (3 inches). Have them measure from the mouse to the rabbit and record that distance (5 inches). Next, have them measure the distance from the rabbit to the cat (4 inches).

3 Let children finish the activity by completing the equation at the bottom of the page.

Activity 2

How Do I Measure Up?

Here's How

1 Have children work in pairs to measure each other's thumb, middle finger, hand (from tip of finger to wrist), and foot length. Instruct them to write down each measurement, using the nearest inch.

2 Next, have them measure and cut the paper strips into lengths that correspond to their own measurements, and label each strip "thumb," "hand," and so on.

3 Have them tape the four strips of paper together end to end to form one long strip and write their name on the strip.

4 When everyone is finished, have children compare the length of each other's long strips. To do this, help children arrange themselves in size order from tallest to shortest. Then have them hang their strips on a bulletin board from longest to shortest. Ask: "Whose strip is longest?" "Does anyone have strips that are the same length?"

Materials

★ 12-inch rulers
★ construction paper cut lengthwise into strips
★ scissors
★ tape
★ pencils and paper

Here's More

Ask children to look around the room and point out objects that they think are shorter than a 12-inch ruler. Measure each object to verify their guesses. After each child has had a turn, show the class a yardstick and explain that it is the equivalent of three 12-inch rulers and measures 36 inches. Ask children to look around the room and point out objects that they think are longer than a yardstick. Measure the objects to verify each guess.

The Jumping Flea

Measure and write how far jumped from  to .

Measure and write how far jumped from to ___ .

Measure and write how far jumped from ___ to .

inches

inches

inches

How far did the flea jump all together?

___ **+** ___ **+** ___ **=** ___

inches   inches   inches   inches

Little Monkey's Tick-Tock Day

Characters

Little Monkey
Grandma Monkey
Happy Hippos
Grumpy Crocodiles

Little Monkey: Tick-tock. It's 12:00.
It's time to eat lunch today.

Grandma Monkey: After you eat, go swing through the trees.
Have fun with your friends and play!

Little Monkey: Tick-tock. It's 2:00. I see my jungle friends.

Happy Hippos: Swing down from your branch
and ride on our backs.
Let's swim to the river's end.

Little Monkey: Tick-tock. It's 4:00.
Our swim is almost done.

→

Grumpy Crocodiles: Jump on our backs for a river ride.
Doesn't that sound like fun?

Little Monkey: We know you want to trick us today.
You can't fool us with your smiles.

Happy Hippos: We're swimming back home this very minute.
Good-bye grumpy crocodiles.

Little Monkey: Tick-tock. It's 5:00.
Bye-bye, hippos! I'll see you soon.

Grandma Monkey: Hello, Little Monkey. It's dinnertime.
Come eat a banana or two.

Little Monkey: Tick-tock. It's 8:00.
May I hear a story tonight?

Grandma Monkey: Of course, Little Monkey.
We'll read a book first,
And then we'll turn out the light.

Little Monkey: Tick-tock. It's 9:00.
The moon is shining bright.
Good night, Grandma.
Good night, jungle friends.
Good night, everyone!

All: Good night!

☆ The End ☆

Little Monkey's Tick-Tock Day

Performing the Play

Use the following suggestions to perform this play with your class.

★ Choose one volunteer to be Little Monkey and one volunteer to be Grandma Monkey. Divide the rest of the class into two groups to be the hippos or the crocodiles. Little Monkey and Grandma Monkey read their parts standing in the front of the room while the rest read their parts from their seats.

★ Follow the instructions below to make the clock. As children hold their finished clocks at their seats, they can read the play aloud in unison. Have children move the hands of the clock to show the corresponding time throughout the play. Whenever the time changes, pause briefly and allow children to move the hands on their clocks.

Making the Clock

Here's How

1 Give each child a copy of the reproducible. Let children color the clock and the hands, then cut them out. (For a sturdier clock, glue the clock hands to lightweight cardboard before mounting them on the clock.)

2 Have children glue the clock to the center of a paper plate.

3 Show children how to use the pencil point to carefully poke the center hole out of the clock.

Skill

Telling Time

Materials

★ Tick-Tock Clock reproducible, page 70
★ dinner-sized paper plates
★ crayons
★ scissors
★ lightweight cardboard (optional)
★ sharp pencil
★ brass fasteners
★ hole punch
★ glue

4 Let children use the hole punch to make a hole at the end of each clock hand. Have them mount the two hands to the clock, placing the big hand underneath the little hand.

Activity 1

What Time Is It?

Materials

★ What Time Is It? reproducible, page 71
★ pencils
★ scissors
★ glue

Here's How

1 Explain that there are different types of clocks. Have examples of both analog and digital clocks available. Ask children to share which type of clock they have in their home.

2 Have children draw the hands on the clocks in the box and write the correct time.

3 Finish the activity by having children cut out the digital clocks pictured at the bottom of the page and glue them beside the corresponding analog clocks in the middle of the page.

Activity 2

Little Monkey's Day

Here's How

1 Guide children through the instructions on pages 67 and 68 to make the Tick-Tock Clock.

2 As a class, turn the hands of the clock to point to each number on the clock. Pause after the hand is moved each time. Ask children to suggest possible activities Little Monkey might have done at different times of day. Encourage children to suggest activities that correspond to the pictures on the clock. Discuss the difference between morning and afternoon.

3 Ask each child to choose one time of day on the Tick-Tock Clock. Give children time to write an original story about what Little Monkey did during that hour. (Let younger children dictate their stories and draw pictures.) After their stories are written, ask children to share what they imagined Little Monkey did.

Materials

★ Tick-Tock Clock reproducible, page 70
★ lined writing paper
★ pencils

Here's More

Have children bring in an item from home that represents an activity they do at a certain time of day. (For example, a toothbrush might represent the hour when children get up in the morning; a ball might represent a time after school when children play.) As they show the class the items they brought, have children move the hands on the Tick-Tock Clock to point to the time of their activity.

Tick-Tock Clock

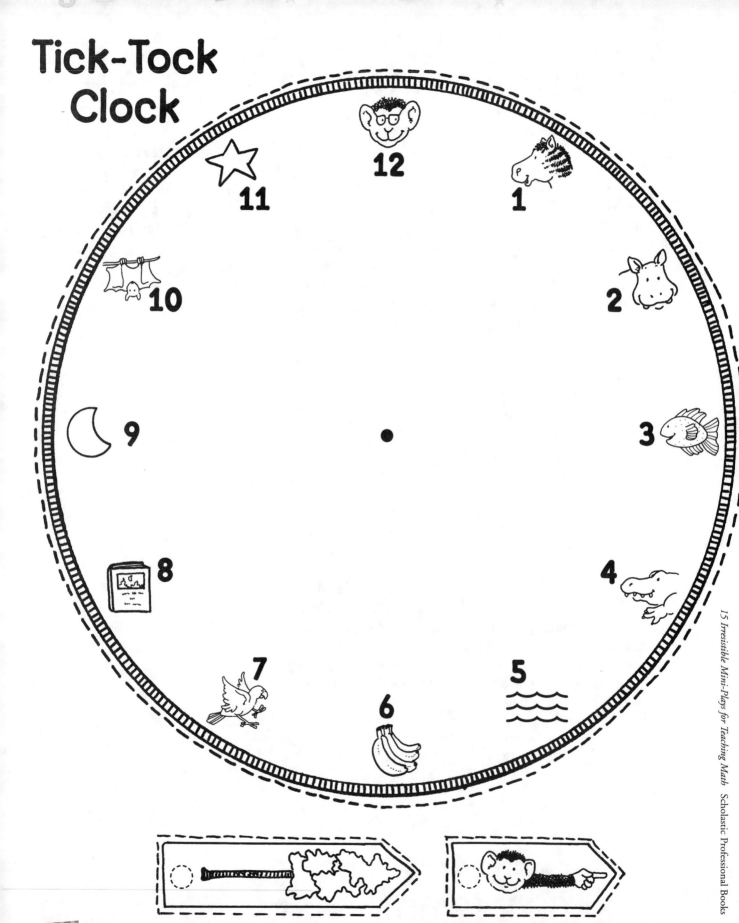

15 Irresistible Mini-Plays for Teaching Math Scholastic Professional Books

☆ What Time Is It? ☆

Draw the hands on the clocks. Write the correct time.

 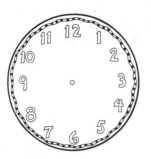  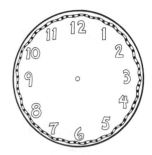

It is

_____ o'clock.

One hour later,
the time is
_____ o'clock.

It is

_____ o'clock.

One hour earlier,
the time is
_____ o'clock.

Cut out the digital clocks at the bottom of the page. Match them with the clocks that show the same time.

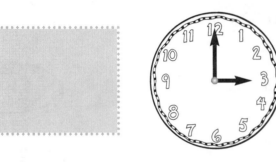

| 8:00 | 4:00 | 12:00 | 6:00 | 3:00 | 1:00 |

Toy Store

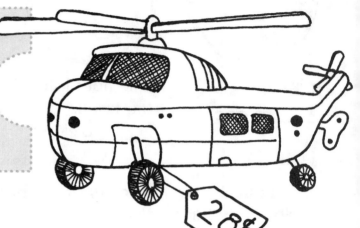

Characters

Toy helicopter   Dinosaur
Toy robot   Shoppers 1 to 4
Toy penguin   Clerk

Shopper 1:   A toy store!
I have money. I'll stop and shop!

Clerk: Look at our price tags.
See if you have the right amount.

Shopper 1:   I want to buy this wind-up helicopter.
It costs 28 cents.
I have 2 quarters.
That makes 50 cents.

Clerk: You have enough! Shop till you drop!

Shopper 1:   I'll take it!
Here are 2 quarters. They are worth 25 cents each.
That makes 50 cents.
The helicopter costs 28 cents.
I will have 22 cents left!

Clerk: Here are 2 dimes and 2 pennies for your change.

⟶

Shopper 2: A toy store!
I have money. I'll stop and shop!

Clerk: Look at our price tags.
See if you have the right amount.

Shopper 2: I want to buy this wind-up robot.
It costs 15 cents.
I have 25 cents.
That's one quarter.

Clerk: You have enough! Shop till you drop!

Shopper 2: I'll take it!
Here is 1 quarter. It's worth 25 cents.
The robot costs 15 cents.
I will have 10 cents left.

Clerk: Here is 1 dime for your change.

Shopper 3: A toy store!
I have money. I'll stop and shop!

Clerk: Look at our price tags.
See if you have the right amount.

Shopper 3: I want to buy this wind-up penguin.
It costs 35 cents.
I have 45 cents.
I have 3 dimes, 2 nickels, and 5 pennies.

Clerk: You have enough! Shop till you drop!

Shopper 3: I'll take it!
Here are 3 dimes. They are worth 30 cents.
Here is 1 nickel.
That makes 35 cents.

Clerk: The penguin costs 35 cents.
Just the right amount!

Shopper 4: A toy store!
I have money. I'll stop and shop!

Clerk: Look at our price tags.
See if you have the right amount.

Shopper 4:   I want to buy this scary looking dinosaur.
     But where is the wind-up key?

Clerk: It doesn't have one.

Shopper 4:   I want to buy it.
     It costs 45 cents.
     I have 50 cents.
     I have 1 quarter. It is worth 25 cents.
     I have 1 dime, 1 nickel, and 10 pennies.
     That makes 50 cents.

Clerk: You have enough! Shop till you drop!

Shopper 4:   Here is 1 quarter. It is worth 25 cents.
     Here is 1 dime. That makes 35 cents.
     Here is 1 nickel. That makes 40 cents.
     Here are 5 pennies. That makes 45 cents!

Clerk: That's just the right amount.

Dinosaur: ROAR!

Shopper 4:   AAAAAAH!

Clerk: I thought there was something
different about that toy!

☆ **The End** ☆

Toy Store

Skill

Money

Performing the Play

Make a tagboard sign that says "Toy Store." Large price tags can be made for each toy. Three tagboard wind-up keys can be taped to the back of the children who perform the part of each toy. The dinosaur doesn't wear a key. The shoppers can each hold the appropriate number of coins. The clerk can provide change. Use the Paper Coins reproducible on page 80.

As the shoppers enter the store, they walk onstage. After they purchase their toys, they pretend to wind up the toys. The toys move or dance offstage with their new owner. When the dinosaur is purchased, it chases its owner off the stage. (The dinosaur is real and isn't a toy.)

Activity 1

Learning Coin Values

Materials

★ Paper Coins reproducible, page 80
★ scissors
★ small container or cup

Here's How

1 Give each child a copy of the Paper Coins reproducible. Make a copy for yourself too. Have children cut out the coins while you do the same.

2 From the extra set, place one of each of the coins in a small container or cup.

3 Choose a volunteer to close his or her eyes and pick one coin from the cup. Discuss the value of the coin with the class. Ask if other coins can be used to make the same value. If so, have children choose a group of coins that add up to the same value.

4 Once children have become familiar with the values of the coins, place several of each coin in the cup. Two or more coins can be pulled out at a time for discussion of value.

Activity 2

Let's Play Store!

Here's How

1 If children are working with different amounts of money than those shown on the reproducible, use correction fluid to cover the amounts on the price tags. Write in the amounts you want to use and then photocopy the revised reproducibles.

2 Give each child a copy of the Let's Play Store! and the Paper Coins pages. Have children cut out the coins.

3 Explain that everyone can cut out pictures of three toys from the toy catalogs to have in their toy stores. Then they will place these pictures on shelves in the store.

4 Have children work in pairs to pretend to buy the toys in each other's toy stores. At first, instruct children to purchase the toys using the exact amounts.

5 The first customer chooses a toy from the other child's store and pays this child the correct amount in coins. (If the customer chooses to buy a picture that's cut out from the catalog, the other child can hand over the purchased "toy.") Then the second child plays customer, chooses a toy from the first child's store, and pays the correct amount. Have children repeat this procedure up to three or four times.

6 Instruct children to purchase the remaining toys, one at a time, with coins that will require change. Have the first child pay his or her partner, and then the partner will count out the change. When finished, children can glue their original toy pictures back in the store.

Materials

★ Let's Play Store! reproducible, page 79
★ Paper Coins reproducible, page 80
★ toy catalogs or advertisements
★ scissors
★ crayons or markers
★ glue

Here's More

Organize a classroom store. Ask children to bring in a small used toy to display on the shelves and label each with a price tag. Duplicate the Paper Coins reproducible on page 80, glue the page to lightweight cardboard, and cut out the coins. The coins can be kept in envelopes that children decorate to use as wallets.

Then have a day when children can pretend to purchase a toy from the store. (Make sure there is at least one toy for each child.) Select names at random to determine the order in which children take turns purchasing their toys and playing store clerk. Repeat the activity to give children more practice counting change and the opportunity to "buy" different toys.

Let's Play Store!

Paper Coins

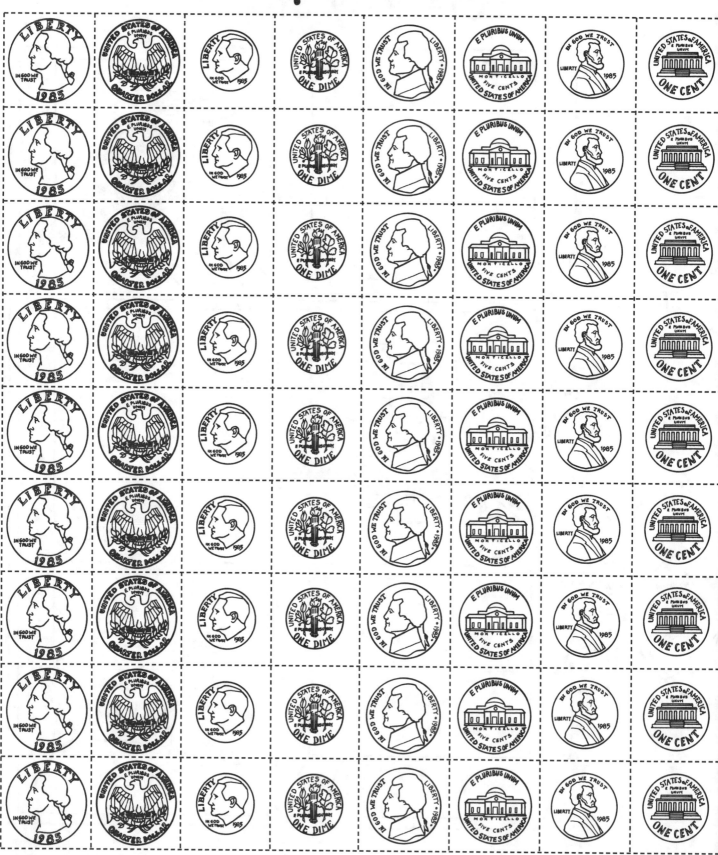

15 Irresistible Mini-Plays for Teaching Math Scholastic Professional Books

Elephant Sleepover

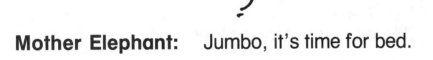

Characters

Mother Elephant   Tiny
Jumbo   Peanut
Chorus   Boomer

Mother Elephant: Jumbo, it's time for bed.

Jumbo: I love having this whole bed to myself.
I can stretch out my trunk, and my feet,
and my big ears.

Chorus: Ding! Dong!

Mother Elephant: Jumbo, your cousin Tiny is here
to spend the night.

Tiny: Hi, Jumbo! Is there room next to you?
It would only be two.

Jumbo: Sure. You sleep on your half of the bed.
I'll sleep on my half of the bed.

Tiny: I'll have one-half. And you'll have one-half. We'll both have equal parts.

Jumbo: Try not to put your trunk on my half.

Tiny: And try not to put your feet on my half.

Jumbo and Tiny: Good night.

Chorus: Ding! Dong!

Mother Elephant: Jumbo, your cousin Peanut is here to spend the night.

Peanut: Hi, Jumbo. Hi, Tiny.
Is there room for me?
Will your bed hold three?

Jumbo: I think so.
I'll sleep on my third of the bed.

Tiny: And I'll sleep on my third of the bed.

Peanut: And I'll sleep on my third of the bed.

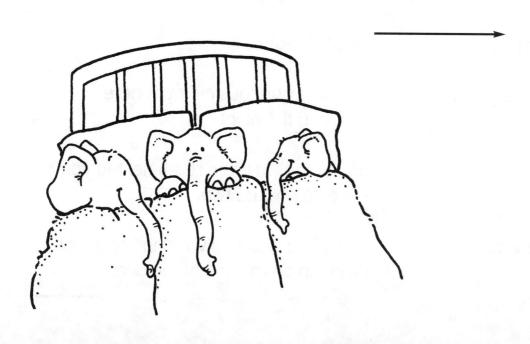

Jumbo: We will each have one-third of the bed.
Three equal parts.
But keep your trunk on your third.

Tiny: And keep your feet on your third.

Peanut: And keep your ears on your third.

**Jumbo, Tiny,
and Peanut:** Good night!

Chorus: Ding! Dong!

Mother Elephant: Jumbo, your cousin Boomer is here
to spend the night!

**Jumbo, Tiny,
and Peanut:** Oh, no! Not Boomer! Boomer's too big!

Boomer: Hi, cousins!
Do you think the bed will hold one more?
It's only four.

Jumbo: Maybe, if we're very careful.
I'll take my fourth of the bed.

Tiny: I'll take my fourth of the bed.

Peanut: I'll take my fourth of the bed.

Boomer: And when I climb in,
I'll take my fourth of the bed.

→

Jumbo: We will each have one-fourth of the bed.
Four equal parts.
But keep your trunk on your fourth.

Tiny: Keep your feet on your fourth.

Peanut: And keep your ears on your fourth.

Boomer: Okay! Here I come!

Jumbo, Tiny, and Peanut: BOOMER! DON'T JUMP ON THE BED!

Chorus: CRASH! BANG! BO-O-O-OM!

☆ **The End** ☆

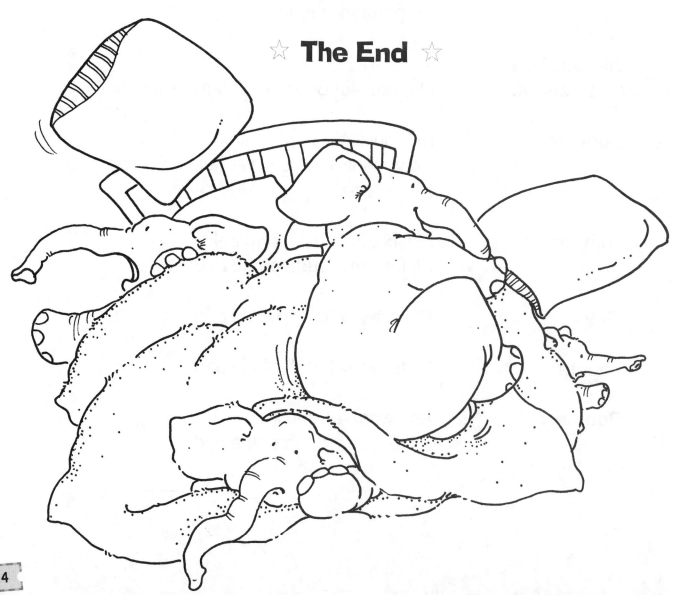

Elephant Sleepover

⭐ Performing the Play ⭐

Children can read this play aloud at their seats, or they can act it out. Choose five children to be the elephants. The mother elephant stands to the side of the "bed," a sheet or rectangular story rug that is placed on the floor. First, Jumbo lies down on the "bed" and stretches out while saying his or her lines. When Tiny arrives, they put a jump rope (or length of yarn) down the middle of the bed to divide it in half. When Peanut arrives, they put two jump ropes down to divide the bed into thirds, and so on. At the end, Boomer pretends to jump on his part of the bed and the bed breaks. For extra fun, let the actors wear their elephant puppets as they perform. (See instructions below.)

⭐ Making the Puppets ⭐

Here's How

1 In advance, cut a 3-inch hole in the center of each paper plate. For younger children, the hole may be slightly smaller.

2 Copy and enlarge two puppet patterns for each child. Have children color and cut out two ears and feet and glue them to the plate as shown. Then have them draw eyes. The puppet is worn on the arm with the hand sticking out for the elephant's trunk.

Materials

⭐ Elephant Puppet Patterns, page 86
⭐ paper plates
⭐ scissors
⭐ crayons
⭐ glue

Elephant Fractions

Activity 1

Materials

★ Elephant Fractions
  reproducible,
  page 88
★ scissors
★ glue

Here's How

1 Give each child a copy of the reproducible. Have children cut out the elephants on the left side of the page.

2 Tell children to glue one elephant onto each shaded part. Instruct them to write the fraction that each picture represents.

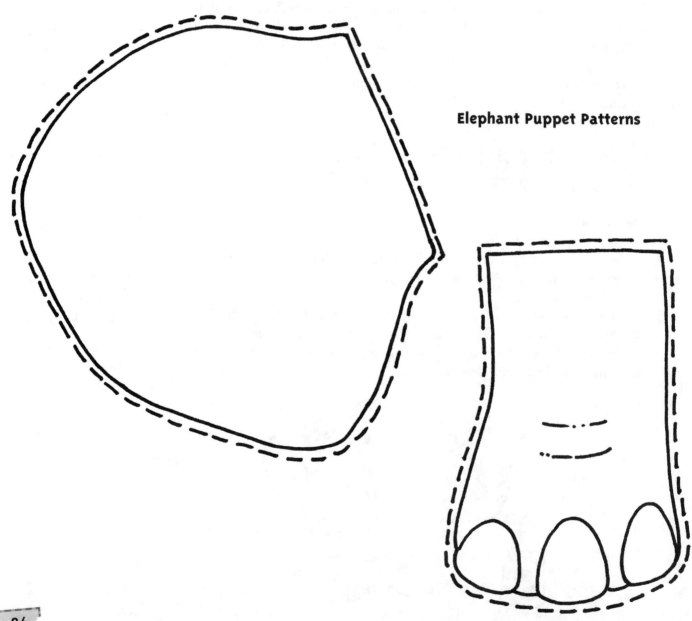

Elephant Puppet Patterns

Activity 2

Fraction Cake Decorating

Here's How

1 Give children each one sheet of construction paper to represent a sheet cake. Discuss the different fractions you are studying.

2 Encourage each child to choose one fraction. Have children fold their paper in halves, thirds, or fourths, according to which fraction they chose. Let them decorate the part(s) of their cake to represent the fractions. Then ask children to take turns sharing the fraction they made.

Materials

★ construction paper
★ scissors
★ crayons
★ stickers or other small items for decorating cakes

Here's More

Play Fraction Fishing Make a classroom set of playing cards using 40 unlined index cards. Leave one side blank on all the cards. Then prepare the other side of the cards as follows:

★ On eight of the cards, draw circles or squares divided into halves with one half shaded. Label these "1/2."

★ On eight other cards, draw circles or squares divided into thirds with one part shaded. Label these "1/3."

★ On eight more cards, draw circles or squares divided into thirds with two parts shaded. Label these "2/3."

★ On eight cards draw circles or squares divided into fourths with one part shaded. Label these "1/4."

★ On the remaining eight cards, draw circles or squares divided into fourths with two parts shaded. Label these "2/4" or "1/2," according to the concept you want to teach.

How to Play (2 or 3 players)

Deal five cards to each player and spread out the remaining cards upside down in the middle. The first player asks one of the other players for a card that matches one in his or her hand. If the second player doesn't have the matching card, he or she says, "Go Fish!" The first player then draws a card from the pile in the middle. If it doesn't match the card requested, it is the next person's turn. If it does match, the player places the matched pair face up on the table and takes another turn. The player who collects the most fraction pairs wins the game.

Elephant Fractions

Put one elephant on each shaded part of the bed.
Then write the fractions.

$$\frac{1}{3}$$

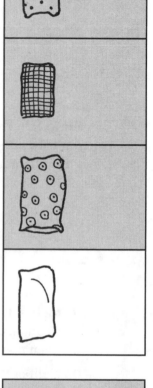

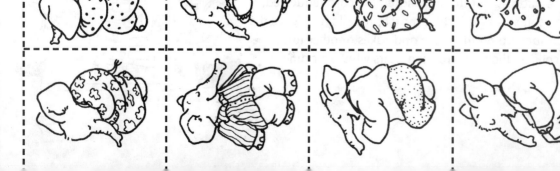

One Little, Two Little, Three Little Pigs

Characters

Little Pig 1	Narrator 1	Wolf
Little Pig 2	Narrator 2	
Little Pig 3	Narrator 3	

Narrator 1: Once upon a time,
there were three smart little pigs.
The first little pig met
a cow selling straw.

Pig 1: Please, Mrs. Cow, may I buy some straw?

Wolf: Sure. Here's my snack—I mean—stack of straw.

Narrator 1: The first little pig built a house.
She put down one big pile of straw.

Narrator 2: Then she put down two small piles of straw.
Next, she added one big pile of straw.

Narrator 3: Then she put down two small piles of straw,
one big pile, two small piles.
Soon the house was done.

Pig 1: What a nice pattern!

Narrator 2:   The second little pig met a farmer selling sticks.

Pig 2:   Please, Mr. Farmer, may I buy some sticks?

Wolf: Certainly. Here's my lunch—I mean—
bunch of sticks.

Narrator 1:   The second little pig built a house.
First, he put down three sticks.
Then he put down two sticks.
Then he put down one stick.

Narrator 2:   Next, he added three sticks,
then two sticks,
then one stick.

Narrator 3:   Three, two, one. Three, two, one.
Soon the house was done.

Pig 2:   What a nice pattern!

Narrator 3:   The third little pig met a chicken selling bricks.

Pig 3:   Please, Mrs. Hen, may I buy some bricks?

Wolf: You bet! Here's my meal—
I mean—wheelbarrow of bricks.

Narrator 1:   The third little pig built a house.

Narrator 2:   First, she put down one red brick.
Then she put down one brown brick.
Then she added one white brick.

Narrator 3:   Red, brown, white. Red, brown, white.
Soon the house was done.

Pig 3:   What a nice pattern!

Narrator 1:   Now the wolf was ready for dinner.
He walked up to the house made of straw.

Wolf: Knock.

Pig 1:   Knock?
You're supposed to go knock, knock, knock.
Knock, knock, knock.
Use patterns, Mr. Big Bad Wolf!
Then you can have your dinner!

Wolf: Patterns? I don't care about patterns.
I just want my dinner! HUFF!

Narrator 2:   As the house blew down, the first little pig
ran out the back door.
She ran all the way
to her brother's house of sticks.

Narrator 3:   Now the wolf was really hungry.
He walked up to the house made of sticks.

Wolf: I want my dinner.
Open up or I'll huff!

Pig 2:   Huff? You're supposed to say,
"I'll huff and I'll puff and
I'll blow your house down!"
Use patterns, Mr. Big Bad Wolf!
Then you can have your dinner!

Wolf: I don't know what patterns are! HUFF!

Narrator 1:   As the house blew down, the two little pigs
ran out the back door.
They ran all the way
to their sister's house of bricks.

Narrator 2:   Suddenly the wolf remembered.
Patterns were things that repeated themselves.
He decided to use patterns to get his dinner!

Narrator 3:   The wolf marched down the road.
Left, right. Left, right.
He came to the house made of bricks.

Wolf: Knock, knock, knock!
Knock, knock, knock!

Pigs 1, 2, and 3:   Who's there?

Wolf: It's me, and I'm using patterns!
Little pigs, little pigs, let me come in!

Pig 3:   Come on in! Dinner's ready for you!

Wolf: Dinner? For me?

Pig 3:   Of course! If you agree to work with us,
we'll fix you dinner every day.

Wolf: How will we work together?

Pig 1:   We want to build houses with patterns.
But we need you to buy the straw,
sticks, and bricks.

Pig 2:   You buy the stuff.
We'll build the houses with patterns.

Pig 3:   Every day we'll cook your dinner.
Is it a deal?

Wolf: It's a meal—I mean—deal!

☆ **The End** ☆

One Little, Two Little, Three Little Pigs

Performing the Play

To perform this play, children can simply read aloud the dialogue. Or let them perform the play as a bigger production complete with costumes and props.

Here's How

1 Assemble the props.

★ **PIGS' HOUSES:** Cut three large house shapes from craft paper and tape to a wall or simply draw the outlines on the chalkboard. (Optional: Assemble a table and chairs and toy dishes for the last scene, when the wolf arrives for dinner at the brick house.)

★ **STRAW:** Gather together several yellow pipe cleaners or drinking straws and wrap with a rubber band to make a "big" pile of straw. Cut pipe cleaners in half to make "small" piles. (Or substitute strips of yellow paper and tape them together.) Make about 16 to 18 piles of each and place in a box.

★ **STICKS:** Cut about 30 to 36 12-inch-long strips from brown construction paper and place in a box.

★ **BRICKS:** Place about 18 to 24 sheets each of red, brown, and white construction paper in a box.

2 Assemble the costumes.

★ **WOLF:** Tie elastic cord to a small foam cup with pipe-cleaner whiskers poking out through the sides.

★ **WOLF DRESSED AS MRS. COW:** The wolf also wears a bell tied to a yarn necklace.

★ **WOLF DRESSED AS MR. FARMER:** The wolf also wears overalls and a straw hat.

★ **WOLF DRESSED AS MRS. HEN:** The wolf also wears a paper headband with yellow or red feathers glued around the edge and an orange or red paper triangle taped inside.

★ **PIGS:** Tie elastic cord to small foam cups that have two pink paper circles glued on the bottom for nostrils.

Wolf

Mrs. Hen

Pig

3 Perform the play.

★ The wolf should always wear its own nose even when dressed up as the cow, farmer, or hen. To give the wolf time to change costumes, allow a slight intermission after each pig builds its house.

★ To build their houses, the pigs can stand in front of the house backdrops and tape the "straw," "sticks," or "bricks" onto each house, following the pattern described in the play. For example, to build the straw house, the pig first tapes up two small piles of pipe cleaners and then adds a big pile on top of these, or to the side. For the stick house, the pig first tapes up three strips of paper grouped close together, then two strips, then one, and so on.

★ In the final scene, when the wolf arrives for dinner at the brick house, there can be a table prepared with dinner waiting for him.

Activity 1

The Pattern Game

Here's How

1 Seat everyone in a large circle on the floor and explain the game to the children.

2 Choose one volunteer to leave the room.

3 Pick one child to be "it." That child will then create patterns for others to follow—for example, clap hands, clap hands, tap knees, clap knees; clap hands, clap hands, tap knees, tap knees. As the pattern gets going, children imitate it.

4 Invite the volunteer to come back into the room and stand in the center of the circle as all children are performing the pattern.

5 Instruct the leader to change the pattern periodically—for example, tap the head with the right hand three times, with the left hand three times, and repeat. Everyone should imitate the new pattern, trying not to make it obvious who initiated it.

The player in the center of the circle gets three chances to try to guess who "it" is. If he or she guesses correctly, the player gets to guess again the next time the game is played. If he or she can't guess, "it" becomes the new player to stand in the middle of the circle.

Building With Patterns

Materials

* Building With Patterns reproducible, page 99
* pencils
* crayons or markers

Here's How

1 Distribute the reproducible to children and have them continue the patterns of houses for numbers 1 to 3.

2 For numbers 4 to 6, discuss how the pigs wanted to build new houses with patterns. Invite several volunteers to draw pattern ideas on the chalkboard.

3 Give children time to design their own patterns on the reproducible, leaving the last two lines blank in numbers 4 to 6. (Have children design their own house shapes and patterns in number 6.)

4 Tell children to exchange papers and try to continue each other's patterns. If a pattern doesn't work, ask children to identify the problem and change the example until the pattern can be continued correctly.

5 Invite children to color their houses if they wish.

Divide the class into groups of six. Ask each group to find ways to use their own bodies or characteristics to create patterns. For instance, they can stand in a row according to short hair, short hair, long hair, short hair, short hair, long hair. Or they can stand boy, girl, boy, girl, boy, girl. Or they can sit, sit, stand, stand, sit, sit. When the groups are ready, have one group position itself in its pattern. Let the other groups guess what the pattern is. Let all groups take turns demonstrating their patterns to the others.

Building With Patterns

Look at the patterns below. Then draw what comes next.

1.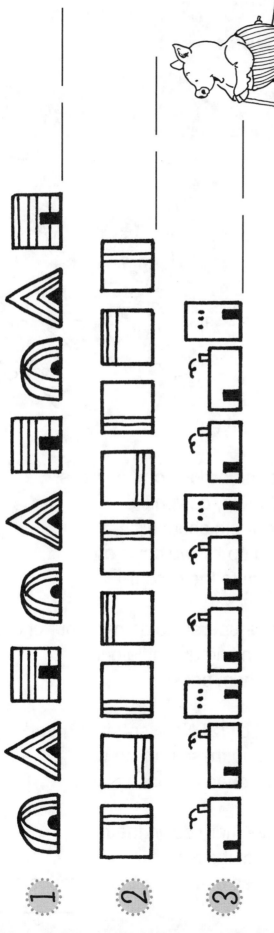

2.

3.

Now build your own houses with patterns. Leave the last two lines blank in each row. Ask a friend to draw what comes next.

4.

5.

6.

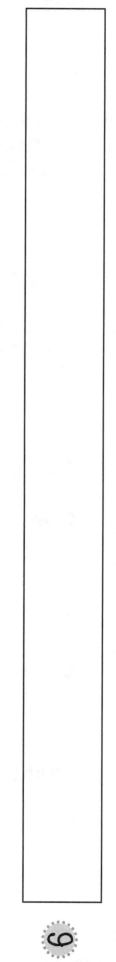

☆ The ☆ Round-up

Cowpokes 1, 2, and 3:   Yippee-yi-yi-yea!!

Cowpoke 1:   I just got an order from the boss.
Now listen up, cowpokes.
Here's our big chance:
We round up twelve cows and
Bring them to the ranch!

Cowpoke 2:   Jingle your spurs! Hold on to your chaps.
We're rounding up cattle and
Bringing them back!

Cowpoke 3:   We found all 12! Now isn't that great!
I'll round up these four cows,
You both round up those eight.

Cowpoke 1:   Let's drive them down the trail!
That's what it's for.
Divide those cattle into three groups of four.

Cowpoke 2: Jingle your spurs! Hold on to your chaps.
We're rounding up cattle and
Bringing them back!

Cowpoke 3: Let's cross this rushing river.
Listen to them moo!
One dozen cattle in six groups of two.

Cowpoke 1: They're kicking up trail dust.
It's getting hard to see!
Divide those cattle into four groups of three.

Cowpoke 2: All 12 cattle
thunder through the gate,
One cow at a time
In a line nice and straight.

Cowpoke 3: Jingle your spurs! Hold on to your chaps.
We rounded up 12 cows
And brought them all back.

Cowpokes 1, 2, and 3: The round-up is done. It's been quite a day!
Let's kick off our boots! Yippee-yi-yi-yea!

☆ The End ☆

The Round-up

☆ Performing the Play

Use the following suggestions to perform this play with your class.

★ Read aloud the play as children sit at their seats and use manipulatives to represent the different groupings of cattle. Explain unfamiliar terms such as *chaps* (a cowboy's leather leggings), and *spurs* (pointy metal objects on a rider's heel, used to urge on a horse).

★ Choose three children to wear cowboy outfits and speak with a western drawl. Twelve volunteers can be the cattle. At the corresponding places in the play, the cowpokes group the 12 cattle into the suggested groups. Encourage the cattle to moo, run in place, and hold their hands on either side of their heads to resemble horns.

Activity 1 — Marshmallow Cows

Skill
Grouping

Materials

★ mini-marshmallows (Stale marshmallows are easier to handle. Dry the marshmallows overnight by spreading them out on a tray.)

★ toothpicks

Here's How

1 Discuss the different types of groupings in the play.

2 Choose volunteers to come to the chalkboard and draw examples of the different types of groupings. (Children may simply draw circles to represent the cows.) Ask the class if there are other ways to divide 12 into different groupings.

3 Divide the class into groups and have each group sit at a different table. Assign each table of children one type of grouping. For instance, children at one table might each make models of "one dozen cattle in six groups of two." Models can be made with toothpicks and marshmallows. Each child's model may vary.

4 When finished, look at the different models with children and discuss the similarities or differences between them.

5 After discussing groupings for the number 12, let children make models for other numbers that have been divided into groups. Before they begin, have volunteers draw samples of groupings on the chalkboard.

Activity 2

The Guessing Game

Here's How

1 Have children work in pairs. Give each child a copy of the reproducible so he or she can cut out a set of cards.

2 The first player secretly chooses one card from his or her set and holds it so it can't be seen. (On the lap is a good spot.) The first player's other cards can be turned upside down.

3 The second player places his or her cards face up. He or she then tries to guess which cow the first player has chosen. The second player can ask questions, such as, "Does your cow have an open mouth?" The first player answers yes or no.

4 The second player discards all the cards that don't fit the description. These cards can be put in one group and labeled "group."

Materials

★ The Guessing Game reproducible, page 105

★ scissors

5 The second player continues asking questions, such as, "Is your cow wearing a bell?" "Does your cow have its eyes closed?" "Is your cow eating hay?" Each time the first player answers, the second player discards another group of cards and labels them "group."

6 Finally, the second player will have only one card left. At this point, he or she asks the player the name of the cow. For instance, "Is your cow named Daisy?" The answer will be correct if the child has discarded the correct groupings of cards.

7 After guessing the first player's card, children can count how many cows are in each group of discarded cards. They can add all the cards in each group which should equal 12.

8 The game can be played again with the players switching roles.

Here's More

Write the song below on chart paper. Choose 12 children to stand at the front of the room. Then have the class sing this song to the tune of "Home on the Range."

> **Oh give me a home**
> **where the 12** [or other number you choose] **cattle roam,**
> **where they moo-o-ove into groups**
> **through the day.**
> **Different groups large or small,**
> **still just 12** [or other number you choose] **cows in all.**
> **Hear the cowpokes sing, Yippee-yi-yea!**

After singing the song, ask a volunteer to suggest one way to arrange the 12 children into groups and direct children to arrange themselves as suggested. Sing the song several more times and give other children a turn. Repeat the activity, singing the song about different numbers, and have children demonstrate possible groupings.

The Guessing Game

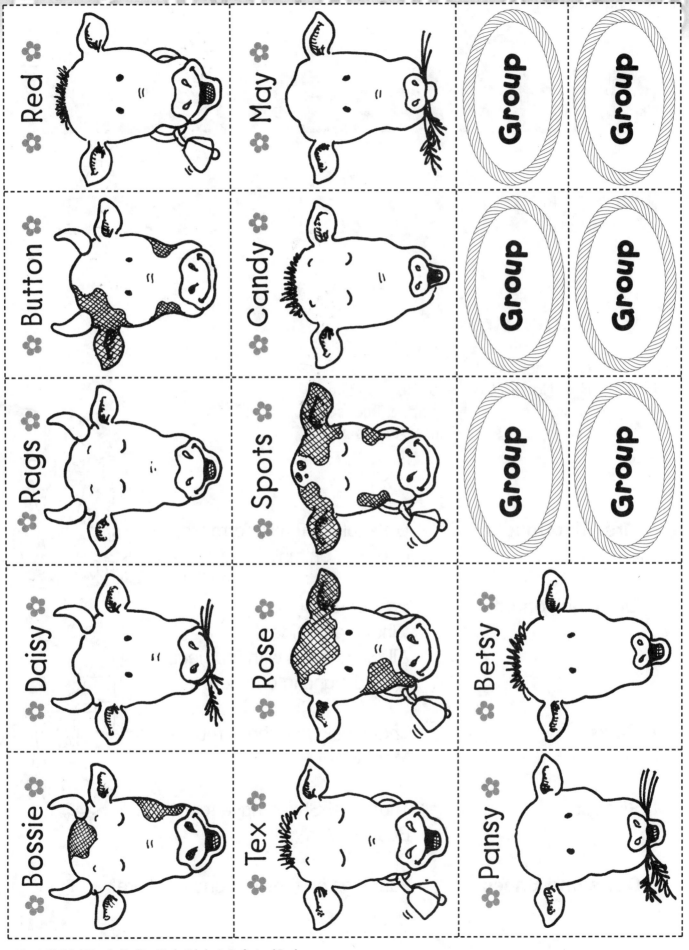

Red

May

Group

Group

Button

Candy

Group

Group

Rags

Spots

Group

Group

Daisy

Rose

Betsy

Bossie

Tex

Pansy

Old MacDonald's Family Picture

Characters

Old MacDonald	Spotted Pigs
Mrs. MacDonald	Spotted Chickens
Cows	Spotted Ducks
Sheep	Three Bears

Mrs. MacDonald: Let's take a family farm picture of all our animals!

Old MacDonald: Ee-I-ee-I-oh!
What a great idea!
All the animals with four legs should stand in one pen.

Cows: That's us! Cows have four legs. Moo! Moo!

Sheep: That's us! Sheep have four legs. Baa-aa! Baa-aa!

Cows and Sheep: Four legs on the floor and no more!

→

Old MacDonald: All the animals with spots
should stand in the other pen.

Chickens: That's us! We chickens have spots.
Cluck! Cluck!

Ducks: That's us! We ducks have spots.
Quack! Quack!

Chickens and Ducks: Spots will do for me and you!

Spotted Pigs: Hey! Wait a minute.
We pigs have four legs and spots.
We belong on both sides.
Where should we stand?

All: In the middle pen.

Mrs. MacDonald: I want to be in the picture too.

Old MacDonald: Ee-I-ee-I-oh! Me too!
                           You're wearing a spotted apron.
                           I'm wearing a shirt with spots.
                           Let's stand with the chickens and ducks.

Three Bears: Hey! Wait a minute.
                           Where should we stand for the picture?
                           We're the Three Bears.

All the animals: THE THREE BEARS?

Old MacDonald: The Three Bears don't belong
                           on Old MacDonald's farm!
                           You're in the wrong story!

Mrs. MacDonald: But since you're here,
                           would you take our picture?

Three Bears: Sure! Smile and say, Ee-I-ee-I-oh!

All: Ee-I-ee-I-oh!

☆ **The End** ☆

Old MacDonald's Family Picture

Performing the Play

Use the following suggestions to perform this play with your class.

★ Read the play aloud while children use the Family Pictures story mat reproducible on page 112.

★ Let children act out the play. Create a Venn diagram by placing two large overlapping yarn circles on the floor (the animals' pens). Each circle should be large enough for students to stand inside. Choose volunteers to be Old MacDonald, Mrs. MacDonald, and the Three Bears. Divide the rest of the class into five groups. As the play is performed, the different characters move to stand inside the correct circles. The Three Bears stand outside the circles.

Let each group of animals make a simple headband from construction paper, glue, and craft materials to identify which animal they are.

★ COW: brown headband with brown horns and ears

★ SHEEP: white headband, white ears, and cotton balls

★ PIG: pink headband with spots, ears, and curly tail

★ DUCK: yellow headband with spots and several small yellow feathers; yellow semi-circle taped inside the headband creates a bill

★ CHICKEN: red headband with spots and several red or brown feathers; orange or red triangle taped inside the headband creates a beak

★ OLD MACDONALD: large paper spots taped to a shirt

★ MRS. MACDONALD: spotted apron made from a sheet of construction paper stapled to a yarn waistband tie

★ THREE BEARS: Each holds a camera made from a small cracker box covered with black construction paper; a large circle glued to the front represents the camera lens

Cow

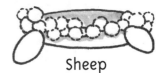

Sheep

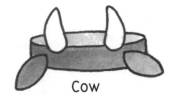

Pig

Duck

Chicken

Old MacDonald

Mrs. MacDonald

Three Bears

Family Pictures

Materials

★ Family Pictures reproducible, page 112
★ crayons
★ scissors

Here's How

1 Distribute a copy of the reproducible to each student. Instruct students to color the pictures of the animals on the bottom of the page and cut out each one.

2 As the play is read aloud, have children place the animals in the correct groupings on the Venn diagram pictured on the story mat.

3 When the play is finished, ask children to explain why they placed the different animals inside or outside each ring. "Are any animals in the middle ring?" "Why?"

All About Me

Materials

★ large sheet of plastic (Use a shower curtain liner or cut open a large, plastic garbage bag.)
★ yarn
★ stapler
★ construction paper
★ markers
★ self-sticking notes
★ pencils

Here's How

1 Make a bulletin board by mounting a large sheet of plastic on the board. Make a Venn diagram on the bulletin board by stapling two large circles of yarn that overlap.

2 Label each ring with a strip of construction paper that describes a specific characteristic that can be compared and contrasted. Some examples include: "I am wearing stripes/I am wearing blue"; "I like fruits/I like vegetables"; "I have a sister/I have a brother"; and "My birthday is during the summer/My age is an even number."

3 Give each student a self-sticking note. Have students write their names on the notes.

4 Ask students to place the notes on the Venn diagram. After the names are on the bulletin board, discuss why students placed their names where they did. Ask: "Why are some names in both rings?" "Where do names go that do not belong in either ring?" "Why?"

5 After the discussion, label the Venn diagram with a new set of characteristics. Ask children to move their names into the correct ring. Repeat this activity as often as you like.

Here's More

Ask children how many pets would be in their own family photograph. (For children who do not have pets, have them think about the pets they'd like to have.) Draw a graph with three columns on craft paper. Label one column "I have fewer than 3 pets"; label the second column "I have 3 pets"; and the third "I have more than 3 pets." Give students each an index card on which they write their name and draw all their pets. (Students who do not have pets may draw their imaginary pets or write "no pets.") When finished, have students tape their index cards to the graph. Then, as a class, compare the different columns. Ask questions such as, "Which column has the most names in it?" "The fewest names?" "Do more children have fewer than 3 pets or more than 3 pets?" "How many pets are there all together?" You might then make Venn diagrams to organize information by groupings, such as "Pets We Wish We Could Have/Pets We Have at Home," or to compare and contrast different characteristics of pets, such as "My pet swims/My pet has 2 legs."

Family Pictures

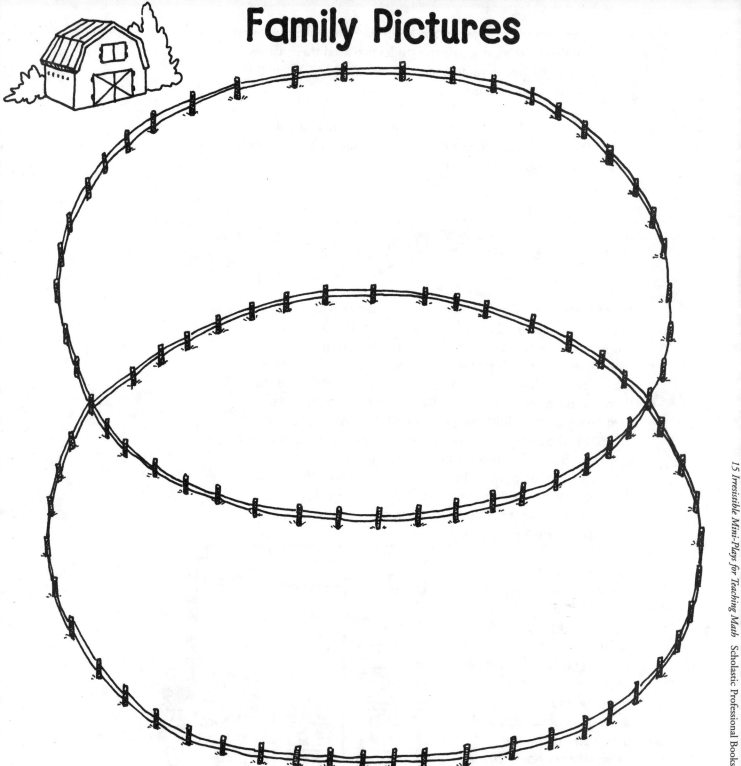

Cows

Sheep

Pigs

Ducks

Chickens

Mrs. MacDonald
Old MacDonald

The Three
Bears